The True Adventures of a Texas Sharecropper Kid

Lonnie L.Willis

authorHOUSE®

AuthorHouse™
1663 Liberty Drive
Bloomington, IN 47403
www.authorhouse.com
Phone: 1-800-839-8640

First published by AuthorHouse 9/10/2009

ISBN: 978-1-4389-9513-7 (e)
ISBN: 978-1-4389-9512-0 (sc)

Library of Congress Control Number: 2009908360

Printed in the United States of America
Bloomington, Indiana

This book is printed on acid-free paper.

For My Mother, Willie Mae Willis, 1902-2003

Without the gracious help and love I received from the Penelope High School class of 1949, I would still be picking cotton.

<u>Prologue</u>

On my thirteenth birthday I picked up a rusty nail from our front yard and scratched my name and the date into a clapboard on the side of our frame house where the afternoon sun was making a scorcher. The grain in the weathered board ran lengthwise, and I had to gouge the nail through each letter and number several times while sweat ran out of my hair into my eyes. I cut deep into the grain, because I wanted my rough-cut sign to last a lifetime. In years to come, maybe when I was dead or famous, I'd come back and stand on this very spot and be glad I had left a mark that connected me with Texas. Like a brand in the hide of an animal, my mark said this place right here, my birthplace on this fixed surface of Texas, was always mine, and if I'd been rich and owned a Kodak I would have snapped a picture of the side of our house where I'd carved my handmade trademark: LEON-13 BIRTHDAY-JUNE 3 1945.

The house burned to the ground, of course. Maybe ten years later Old Man Mose, characterized even by my red-headed but peaceable mother as "the meanest old man," widely notorious in our county for wearing black and delighting in fires, torched a fence row after herding his turkeys onto another man's maize field. It was told he'd made no move to extinguish the traveling flames even as they reached the house which had stood vacant since my mother and my grandfather and I moved away for good. I now imagine him gleefully edging near to the tinderbox and sweating underneath his black frock while the sparks flew upwards and the chimney collapsed into the ashes. Each time my thoughts leap beyond the burning house, I speculate on how the impulses of my thirteenth year were a whirlwind of longings for a past burdened with romantic daydreams about whatever lay ahead.

Truth was, the emotions guiding the posting of my name on the side of a frame house in the apocalyptic year of the Second World War had matured in the midst of conditions found among the country poor. As the Christmas season approached with oranges and stripy candy and a tin drum in my seventh year, my father suddenly had a heart attack and died. Subsequently, my mother, totally ill-prepared for widow-hood, and I, grossly unfitted for life among the toughs, set out from my birthplace on several years of wanderings, living among a variety show of quaint but affable kinfolk, my mother working odd jobs that fell to a woman with six grades of schooling. Going on a barefoot walkabout in the wilderness is a metaphor I respect. It's no surprise to recognize myself at the slippery slope of puberty, balanced in the hot Texas sun with a nail in my hand and carving in my heart, prepared to celebrate our coming home again to the familiar home-place on the D.D. Hickman Ranch.

Nearly everybody in Hill County referred to those three sections of central-Texas hill country, some two-thousand-plus acres of scrub, mesquite, and blackland soil, as the Hickman Place, named for D.D.

Hickman, or "Mr. David," as we all knew him. My grandfather, however, insisted on denominating those acres the "Hickman Ranch." His theory was that a handful of grown men and one boy chasing several hundred head of whiteface cattle all over creation made them "a dadgum ranch." Other folks maintained that if you rounded up the cattle on foot, whistling and yelling them into the corral without a remuda of horses, and raised cotton and hay between roundups, you had to call them the "Hickman Place." When I was thirteen years old and expected to be a real cowboy like Gene Autry, I threw in with my grandfather, and said I'd been born on the Hickman Ranch.

The following is my story, how I lived in good times and bad times, and why nobody can tell it but me.

Chapter 1

FOUR POUNDS SOAKING WET

Work? Considering my experience with the subject in a few more years, how could work be the theme of my First Big Day? Well, on the day I was born, 3 June 1932, there were mobs of folks, some wearing countrified overalls, some fixed up in print dresses, some swelled out in white ducks and straw boaters, looking for work and not finding it. My First Big Day came on the high tide of the Great Depression, a time when twelve million Americans were bereft of work. Jobless and homeless, men and women dropped out of all walks of life, from every social and economic class, and took to the open road looking for a wage or a handout. A high water mark of this period was an affair called the "Bonus March," which was 20,000 World War I veterans from all over America marching on the nation's capitol and petitioning for pre-payment of their war bonuses, not promised by Congress until 1945, when many of them would no longer be eligible for a bonus but be dead. Thus it was that on 3 June 1932, my First Big Day, twenty thousand restless and jobless veterans were arriving in Washington, D.C. and camping on the Capitol lawn and raising a shanty town on the muddy Flats across the Potomac. In the cross-hairs of General Douglas MacArthur, the exhausted men waited to hear the good word from their Congress, a sign that a bonus bill would put some cash in their pockets to take home to their wives and kids. However, President Hoover had already given General MacArthur his orders: if the veterans raised hell, move 'em out. Personally unmoved by this clamor, I spent the day in a shoebox.

My arrival deserved coverage in *Life* magazine if it hadn't waited four more years to begin publishing. It was a country-doctor story, missing the ugly weather subplot. No mud, no blizzard, the June weather warm and dry, big old Texas sun shining down, not a cloud in the sky. Once Dr. Barnes received word in his office in Hubbard that I was arriving, he grabbed his black bag and drove his Model-A Ford through the sunny day, passing along the eleven miles of country roads out to the Hickman Ranch, to find my mother being tended by an older neighbor woman, Mrs. Lees, the mother of a two-year-old son, Bobby, who gleefully welcomed my arrival. Playmates were scarce in his yard. He announced a friendly greeting to me in baby talk and was sent to play by himself in another room.

Both my mother and Mrs. Lees were in a state of surprise as I wasn't due for another month or so. Dr. Barnes, too, thought I was lacking in patience. There had been no prediction of this early delivery. Little prenatal care existed for poor country women at the time. They barely had money to pay the doctor, anyway.

"Premature by a month," Dr. Barnes announced. "Four pounds, soaking wet."

"Littlest baby I ever delivered," he continued. "Do you have a shoebox around here you don't need?" That shoebox was to be my private bed until I inched up and spread out enough to fill a Washington State applebox, smelling like the Giant Red Delicious.

The applebox and I grew up together. I know for sure my sharecropping, Depression-plagued father couldn't write a check for a Sears Roebuck crib or push home a comfy Victorian Perambulator with spring shocks for me to loll in. Actually, those luxuries didn't cross my mind. I was jubilant when my mother tossed a pillow and me into the applebox, and sang popular songs to me. Today I can't recall any 1930's titles, but I remember in later years my mother speaking of her aggravation when I repeatedly cried to hear "the song about a battery." In any case, Momma pushed the applebox back and forth on a linoleum rug to the tune of homemade music.

Wheels came to my applebox shortly after I moved into the various beds of my parents and my teenage sisters. Because my daddy held a family prayer session at the stroke of nine o'clock each evening, I began wearing cowboy-and-Indian pajamas with a drop seat in the rear. At the word "Amen" I'd be lured through the darkened kitchen to the back room where two beds belonged to Maidie and Lucy, both in their teens. Since both sisters told stories about little boys who either were whisked away by skeletons and never heard from again or had body parts sliced off when sharp objects fell on them, I required more company at bedtime than was found in the applebox. At the age of three I hammered four blackstrap-molasses-bucket lids onto the four corners of the box and created a wobbly cart for hauling bricks, tools, model-T steering wheels, wire, and empty snuff glasses tossed off by my grandfather.

3

Somewhere in my fourth year I stumbled onto a wondrous treasure: a single roller skate. Right away I found I could unscrew the nut securing the heel section to the toe section and have two sets of wheels that spun on tiny, oiley steelballs. After a frustrating set-to of pounding with a sledgehammer on the ball-housings in a frenzied attempt to free the steelballs, it dawned on me that I had the machinery for a scooter. I located a section of a two-by-four in my cart and nailed the two sections of the skates to either end, then emptied the applebox and secured it endwise onto one end of the two-by-four with sixpenny nails. Once a broomstick steering lever was nailed to the box, I began pumping and skateboarding across the hardpacked front yard, terrorizing white Leghorns and Rhode Island reds as I whistled through their peckings and scratchings.

Typical of biographies of great persons like George Washington and Abe Lincoln is the transforming effect on a youthful country lad by his introduction to the larger world inhabited by the worldly-wise. It was just such contacts that brought about the final separation from my applebox. Like any small boy, I longed at that time to accompany Daddy when he went off to his work. My daddy was a tenant farmer and it was up to him to get the picked cotton from the fields to the gin, where wagon-loads of picked cotton were suctioned up into the compressor and compacted into bales which were then graded and bought by cotton jobbers. That whole process was a fascinating one, especially for a five-year-old country boy. It began with a ride into town atop a wagon-load of cotton drawn by two bay-colored mules who took so much time I'd burrow into the cotton with bare feet, and pop open cotton seeds and eat the crisp little nuts from inside that tasted like buttered pecans. My mother told me not to eat the seeds because, she warned, they caused women to lose their babies, but I didn't see any harm in that. They did make my fingers yellow.

At the gin, the biggest building of lumber and tin anybody ever saw, each wagon waited in line for its turn to pull up into the dusty, cotton-smelling alleyway where men nosed the dangling and chuffing vacuum cylinders over the cotton and sucked it up and up until only a few hard, green cotton bolls rolled about on the bottom of the wagon. After the ginning was done, Daddy drove the wagon uptown and tied the mules in the shade of some trees behind Mr. Priddy's grocery store.

Mr. Clark Priddy was a kind man who wore a grocer-man's white apron and always gave me stick candy while he and my daddy talked over our groceries and the amount of the bill. As a usual thing I'd kill time by sitting on sacks of flour in the back of the store and watch sparrows that flew through cracked windows and built nests among the rafters. One day, however, Daddy was deep in talking, and he gave me a dime and told me to walk up the street to Mr. Kiett's drugstore and buy myself a vanilla ice cream cone.

The drugstore was open to the street because it had big ceiling fans keeping all the people at the soda fountain cooled off, and the black and white tiles on the floor chilled my bare feet. Just inside the entrance stood a rack of magazines and comic books. It was the first such display I'd ever been free to inspect all by myself, and I walked up to the exhibit of colorful magazines as if I were controlled by Fate. There were pulp magazines, their slick covers illustrated with ships and airplanes, some pictured cowboys with big hats and sixshooters. Other covers had men in masks and women in not much of anything. But the comic books I saw made me forget the world as I knew it.

I was captivated by the shiny covers and colored panels inside the comics, and I knew I had to own one. I selected a comic book titled *Tip Top Comics*, which featured a funny hillbilly in clodhoppers who was being bothered by a blonde girl in a torn skirt. I took the book to the counter and, lucky for me, it only cost my dime.

Outside again, I thawed my chilly feet on the warm sidewalk and let the joy of ownership spread over me. *Tip Top Comics* itself was grand enough; the four-color illustration of Li'l Abner pursued by Daisy Mae on the cover delighted my eyes. But the comic book was the first thing I'd ever chosen, walked right up to an adult behind a marbled counter, and laid down my dime, and bought all by myself. I felt proud, and I wanted to share that feeling with Daddy. I'd intended to return to Mr. Priddy's store, but my five-year-old attention span was abruptly blind-sided by a racket from the pavement just beyond the entrance to the drugstore. A crowd had gathered while I was shopping the magazine rack, and in the middle of the people was a shouting man. I was probably the shortest person on the sidewalk, so I edged myself among the grownup men and women until, clutching my *Tip Top Comics,* I occupied the front row of a sidewalk revival. The shouting man, no hat, and no coat, but wearing a white sweat-stained shirt, was holding a spread-open Bible in one hand, the two halves of pages dipping and rising like wings. He gestured violently with his other hand like you'd swat at flies. I could tell that he was hot. His face was red, and sweat beaded his forehead and ran off down his face and made the collar of his shirt wet. You could tell the book he held was important, because he kept on jabbing it with his fingers. His voice also grabbed my attention, stunned me, rising and falling in a fascinating rhythm so that sometimes he seemed unable to get his breath, him gasping like. I hoped he didn't fall over, though I wondered what that would be like to see it..

I looked at the faces of people around me. Some of the people looked the way Momma did sometimes when she said she "got carried away." A few of the men looked angry, and they moved away along the pavement, probably so they couldn't hear the words he was crying out. His words didn't sound like the words I heard everyday, but the powerfulness of his voice and his gesturing seized and clutched at me like the bodiless hands in stories my sisters told me in the dark. Scared, I eased out of the crowd and began to run along the street toward my daddy. The man's voice carried after me, and the last words I heard were, "Jeeesus! Jeeesus!"

One day in the next week I parked my scooter in the shade of a cedar tree in our front yard and pulled Daddy's King James Bible out of my apple-gearbox. For reasons I didn't give thought to at the time, the street man had lodged in my imagination, maybe because he'd topped the excitement of my trip to the gin, to Mr. Priddy's grocery, to the drugstore and the comic books. Perhaps the mystery surrounding the man's words, his heated intensity, his voice and physical drama in such a public arena, all kept alive in my mind's eye that sweating man in shirt sleeves, the rolling voice, the punching fingers on the Bible. At any rate, I eased into that role.

I laid the Bible on the top of my apple box, opened it to pages covered in words I couldn't read good, and propped it against the guiding lever of the scooter. I took up my stand in the dust near the scooter and surveyed an unsteady audience of chickens, some coming, some going, some chasing grasshoppers. I began to wave my arms and gesture wildly. At the top of a five-year-old's register I began to preach to the multitude of chickens.

"Jeesus! Jeesus! Uhn, I think he'll be here Saturday! Watch out behind your backs, you ugly old sinful livers! Uhn, Jeesus got your ugly necks in his watch-pocket! They ain't no hidey places gonna save you! Uhn, Hell is down there! Oh, Jeesus! Jeesus! Uhn, all fall down and break your stingy necks! Hell gonna get you! So, shut up about cars! Shut up about air rifles! Shut up about the picture show! Uhn, Shame on you sinners! Oh, Jeesus, you'all better watch out!"

Somehow I could not break a sweat, hot as it was in the yard, and I felt my performance was breaking down in that category. I did achieve some success with getting a rhythm going in my voice by alternating gasps with my breathing with outright screams on the "Jeesus!"

After an especially artful scream, I became aware of someone standing behind me.

"Leon, whatcha doing?"

The voice was that of Bobby Lees, my playmate from down the road. He was standing outside the shade, barefoot, hands in the pockets of his overalls. He had a big grin on his face as if he'd caught me kissing my dog.

"Uhn, preaching, I guess," I said. I wasn't really sure what I was doing. But, whatever it was, it embarrassed me in some way that I couldn't put it into words, and probably looked to Bobby, shamefaced. I put the Bible away and shoved the scooter out among the grazing chickens. They flew and scattered as if caught in a cyclone. My applebox had set me up, I thought, for something that was a mystery to me.

Most of my culture over my first five years bubbled within a blend of loving family. My early health had been chancy, caused by "rickets," for lack of healthy nutrients in my diet. My family ate tons of cornbread, crumbled into sweet milk. Once when an infant I gave Momma a fright while she was holding me with one arm and churning butter with the other hand. She glanced down at me to find my face had turned, in her words, "as black as an old shoe." Running with me in her arms out into the field where my dad was plowing, she stumbled over the furrows, but discovered I had returned to a healthy color before she got to him at the plow. Likely I only needed a good shaking. My near-death episode went unexplained for years until some ancient woman's diagnosis satisfied my mother: "a case of black hives."

Chapter 2

DADDY AND MR. ROOSEVELT

Even when I was a little bitty kid playing in the dirt in a ditch I wondered why my daddy wanted to be a share cropper. I'd push my toy cars along a road I'd scraped in the dirt while staying out of the way of Momma and Daddy chopping cotton in a nearby field, and the sun blistered down so I'd seek the odd shade cast by the bank of the ditch and think it must be misery out in the field working under that sun. Momma and Daddy sweated through their shirts and underneath their hats, and I was in some shade playing. Why did Daddy, I wondered, want to be a share cropper and sweat in the field instead of own a grocer store where we bought cold drinks and watermelons?

Well, as I got older I learned there was less to being a share cropper than wish-and-want and more to must-and-ought. My learning experience grew along as I did so that by the time Daddy was gone a few material possessions of his came to me as material statements defining the small choices which, put together, created the web of necessity within which my daddy "chose" to be a share cropper.

The meaningful relics I now own are a set of working man's tools. There are a hammer, a pair of pliers, a carpenter's rule, and an accounts book. It's the last item, the accounts book with the front cover loose and the back cover missing, that tells me something about who my daddy was before me and, more important, reveals the fateful choices he did make that created his future.

Three and a half by six inches in width and length, the book, a lined memorandum book really, contains maybe fifty pages, a few chipped along the edges, but most of them covered in my dad's awkward handwriting and spelling. Numbers spell out the sums of things: costs of items bought; lists of days worked; weights of feed for cattle; totals of cotton weighed, bales taken to gin; amounts of money owed. Sometimes his totals were wrong. He had trouble with "carrying over" when the catalog of numbers went long. His misspellings also reveal a want of formal schooling: "dayes Work in Corn;" "one Barel Flower;" "Pottato." One itemized list of purchases in Mississippi on March 9, 1901, and written in another's hand, included the sale and cost of the accounts book itself, and seems to be a list of necessities for setting himself up in farming.

1 B Bridle	*1*
1 Single Tree	*15*
1 Clens (?)	*15*
1 Plow Bolt	*10*
2 Daisy Paint (?)	*110*
1 Collar Pad	*35*
1 Pr Shoes	*250*

2 Pr Overalls	*150*
& Hose	*40*
11 Yds Stripe Cot (?)	*70*
This Book	*10*

I assume from these purchases and similar ones over the following months that my daddy was of a mind to settle down as a farmer, maybe grow a family; he wedded Susan Melissa Stroud in the following year. On the inside cover of his brandnew memorandum book he wrote with a pencil: "L.L. Willis and S.M.Willis Their Property." I've often thought Daddy showed an unusual masculine generosity of mind by giving equal billing to his first wife.

But what on earth did my daddy mean when he pencilled that grand inscription inside his accounts book? What could he ever know of "property"? On the one hand he may have intended to claim the book itself as a site for his and Susan Melissa's record of joint investments in their marriage. They would demonstrate a managed budget on its pages, show their debits on one page, their credits on the opposite page. Use black ink, use red ink. At the end of the year, tote it all up in black. On the other hand, did he invest ten cents in a neat and tidy little book in which he and Susan Melissa would be supposed to keep an accurate tally of investments in acres of loam-rich Mississippi bottom lands, of spermy bulls and fertile heifers bought and sold, of government mules put to work hauling timber to a stripping mill, a summary, in short, of their rise to wealth? Was this to be the document of their American Dream? Or, within reason, a Mississippi Dream?

In fact, the document is more nightmare than dream. The words "work" ("dayes Work") and "borrow" ("Barrowed") are so ubiquitous in the book they stick its pages shut like nails in the door of the poor house. My dad could not have imagined on the day he thumbed those fifty blank pages and pipe-dreamed a record of a happy future that he was going to produce a canon of share-croppers' tales of woe. This slim text is a testament to a bullheaded tenant farmer's month-by-month struggle to keep his head above the grave.

There is no evidence in the accounts book that my daddy ever owned anything more than some tools, a few farm implements, the overalls on his back, a bunch of kids, and his labor. In all his life he never owned a house he lived in, nor did he ever claim either mortgage or deed to the land he farmed. Daddy conceived me in an unpainted tenant house which he got "rent free," the fee compensated by his labor on the land. The truth is my daddy never "owned," he always "owed." Even on the day he purchased the little book, he bought it "on credit." The dime for it sits like an orphan at the very end of the list of charges for shoes, overalls, and farm equipment. Total: $8.05. It was sometime later he wrote in pencil beside the charged items: "Paid." And lest that suggest he'd come to grips with his pocketbook, twenty-six days later he borrowed $8.00, and a few years later the accounts book shows my daddy, now married with children, borrowing money from his mother.

Daddy's serial indebtedness doesn't mean he was an idle ne'er-do-well. The truth was otherwise. This book of memoranda is a *work-book* in a literal sense, pages upon pages recording days working in exhaustive, tedious repetition. Two passages out of many illustrate the common practice of tenant farmers working in day labor as part of their responsibility to the landowner. It was usual for my dad to keep a record of days he worked for Mr. David Hickman, on whose land the Willis family lived. Thus, he first titles one page, "David Hickman Worked dayes;" then he lists kinds of work for the week, revealing that he jumped about among "caried hay," "plowed," "haluld Wood," and--simply--"corn." Another job summary, "DD Hickman Work," shows that for a week's "Hay hauling" and "Plowing" he earned $7.50.

My dad's memoranda make one thing perfectly clear: at least as early as 1921 he had sold his soul to the Hickman Ranch. The little book defines in cruel detail the Southern concept of sharecropping as it was practiced in Texas during his lifetime and still within my own years on the land. His itemized debts, weighings of picked cotton, listings and dates of cotton bales, totals of the cotton seed for planting, the hull and meal for cattle, the seed corn, all the necessities for raising crops which were provided by the landowner, these details register the fact that my daddy clung to the bottom rung of tenant farming. To be sure, the devil was in the cotton patch. The sharecropper, trailed by a wife and kids, was the man on the bottom of Texas farming, working the land "on halves." The landowner provided the "furnish," and the labor came from men like my daddy who gave half the yearly income to the owner at season's end. Thus, he painstakingly records the bales of cotton he took to the gin and totes up their weights after they were compressed.

Sometimes he notes the date of his first bale of the season. Even in my teenage years it was still customary in Hill County for the farmer who brought in the first bale of the season to haul it uptown in Hubbard and unload it in the Main and Magnolia Street intersection, upend it there as a sign to folks steering their Fords and Buicks along Main that the cotton season was underway, and, sides that, he was the best cottonpickin' farmer that ever poked seed in God's blackland earth. The cotton jobbers paid a premium for that first bale, and one year my own dad brought in the first bale and got his name in the *Hubbard City News*. Probably that was not his usual luck, for in 1924 his first bale was recorded on 25 August, a late start for summer. More of a custom, I fear, was his linking up the cotton crop with his debts. For example, in 1921 he begins a page with "Money Barred of D.H." The total money he "Barred" over three months came to $63.25. The second half of the page documents the weights of five bales of cotton: 612 pounds, 602, 576, 575, 583. Obviously these transactions are too far in the past for me to conjure the balance or imbalance of the in-goes and out-goes. However, I know my daddy never grew rich at this game, nor did I know anyone who did. And I do have a clear recollection that in the mid-to-late 1940s my mother, my grandfather, and I survived by day labor on the same Hickman Ranch with a joint annual income in the neighborhood of six or seven hundred Texas dollars.

Speak in all justice what you will about the wicked system of tenant farming, I must say in fairness that the partnership--and it was in some crucial ways--between Daddy and "Mr. David" was one of mutual esteem. I believe my dad thought it was just. Doubtless by the time he came to Texas he had submitted to his social and working conditions. He knew he was bound to the land. But equally was his employer tied to the land. The bossman's own father, also D.D. Hickman, had plunged into the land gamble on a big scale in central Texas during the decade following the Civil War, finally reckoning the Hickman's property to be the largest in Hill County. So what does one do with all that land in the Country of Twenty

Acres, Two Mules, and a Cow? Working more than three sections of land that wanted to bust out all over with prickly pear and mesquite, and encourage Texas cows to be fat on mesquite beans, demanded such a quantity of hands that entire families were hired and moved onto the place. Thus, the families of Morgans, Carraways, Vardemans, Hammers, Pasleys, and Willises ended up with a generation of kids who only knew whatever they learned on the Hickman Ranch. And Mr. David dealt as fair a hand to Luther Willis as their positions allowed within an agricultural system which bound the owners of land to large families of field workers who knew God made their hands to fit the handles of plows. For at least two decades my father planted and counted in the language of cotton on the Hickman Ranch, and when he died Mr. David anguished over the fate of the wife and the kid.

I see my photos at that age, and there I stand wearing Dickies overalls, ears poking out like handles on a drinking cup, and my mouth slacked open as if I had an IQ of one-half my body temperature. Not quite ready to ambush a stagecoach. Maybe that country boy not-quite-done look also explains my dad's gentleness with me, despite his physical presence and his outlaw-like appearance with bushy mustache and black hat.

My earliest serious memory of Daddy has me watching him chop wood. There was a wood pile beyond the fence bordering our front yard, close enough to the front porch so firewood could be stacked on the far end, ready for carrying to the stove inside the house. Greenish mesquite limbs and stout pin oak branches lay heaped together near an area littered with wood chips. A log, like a hewn tree, rested in the middle of the litter of chips and bark. Daddy leaned lengths of those branches or young tree trunks or cedar posts with shredding bark against the log, held them in place with a foot, and chopped the limbs against the log with blows of the axe that made swift, deep gashes and flung sweet-smelling chips all around. He flung the cuts of stove wood onto a pile, and I carried two chunks at a time and stacked them on the porch.

My dad chopped with a double-bitted axe, the shiny blade edges honed sharp as sword blades. The axe fascinated me because I liked to watch it make the chips fly. It was too heavy for me to handle, but I sliced twigs along its blade when Daddy left the axe stuck in the log for a few minutes. He lectured me, of course, on the dangers of playing with an axe.

"It's easy to cut off a finger with an axe," he warned. "Or drop it on your foot and chop off a toe." That caused his features to wrinkle up in a caricature of pain. "That's why you always carry an axe this way in case you lose your grip on it." He then showed me how to clasp the helve just behind the heavy axe blade, but my hand was too small to go around it so he held one end of the handle and let me pretend to carry it. "And don't ever let me catch you playing with the axe, you hear?"

Sometimes when the field work was laid by, Daddy cut down young trees along the creeks, and trimmed and stacked them between stakes he drove into the ground. He measured the trimmed logs into precise cubic feet, or cords, for Mr. David, who then sold cord wood to people who drove mule teams into the bottoms and piled the wood into their wagons. For each cord of wood my dad cut and staked he was paid a dollar, and he was such a good woodsman he could cut more than a cord a day. It was productive work when he was not in the fields and the weather was cool with winter coming on.

Momma would sack up some biscuits and fried salt bacon, and we'd take my dad his dinner down on the creek. His coat always lay across a post oak he'd chopped down, because he heated up cutting wood, and he'd take off his black hat and place it beside the coat. Usually when he chopped wood he wore high-topped boots like lumberjacks wore, laced up almost to his knees, because they protected his legs in the brush. I loved playing on the cords of wood and running about among felled trees while my parents ate biscuits and talked. The smell of the damp creek bottom and new-cut wood chips was pleasant to me.

One day my dad was chopping wood down on the creek, and my mother was making peanut butter and smashed banana sandwiches for my lunch. Suddenly he stepped up on the back porch and sat down with his feet on a step.

"Oh, Jane," he called out his name for my mother. "Bring that turpentine bottle out here if you can find it."

"What's the matter?" she called out through the screen door. "We don't have your dinner ready yet." She leaned out the door.

"Come help me get my boot off, "I heard my dad say to her.

"Oh, good gracious alive!" My mother stepped out and closed the door behind her.

I licked peanut butter and smashed banana off my fingers and went to the door. I saw my mother bending over Daddy's left foot, unlacing his lumberjack boot. A deep cut was gashed in the toe of the boot and blood was oozing from the gash in the leather. I had never seen that much blood before so it was kind of exciting to be there.

"Stay back, Baby," he said. "Your mother's going to put turpentine on my toe."

She slipped the big leather boot off, and we saw blood had soaked Daddy's sock.

"What in the world!" my mother said. "You better have some coal oil on that or you'll get blood poisoning sure as I'm standing here." She brushed past me, hurried inside.

Momma brought the fat, glass coal oil jug off the kitchen stove, and while she nursed off the blood-soaked sock and poured coal oil on the bloody toe, Daddy told us how he'd lifted the axe up over his shoulder to strike near the bottom of a mesquite trunk but it tangled in a low- hanging branch and twisted out of his hand. The axe fell blade first on his boot.

He held his bare foot up so my mother could bandage it with a strip from a flour sack. The ruined boot lay on the porch like one of my mother's chickens after she'd wrung its neck. As my mother wrapped the toe, Daddy looked at me and winked one eye without my mother seeing.

"Baby, didn't I tell you about playing with that axe?"

By the time I'd reached five years, I could count on one hand the number of little tin cars made in Japan I'd owned and drove through squishy puddles and around dirt roads I graded at the corner of our house. Mostly my parents couldn't humor me with boughten toys, which they couldn't afford. Once, though, my dad bought me a grand toy: a big red tricycle. I think he had seen the spectacle I made among the chickens in the yard with that home-made scooter and realized every kid needed some kind of cycle. When he left one morning in the wagon to go into Hubbard, he also left a feeling of mystery in the kitchen with my mother. There had been whispers enough to arouse my curiosity. All through the day I stayed in the house near my mother.

"What were you and Daddy whispering about?"

"I can't tell you, or it wouldn't be a surprise," she said, forgetting the risk implicit in a word like surprise. "Why don't you scoot on out and play?"

That Saturday passed slower than a bad cold.

A dirt road came over a faint rise after it passed the big red barn, then dipped and curved behind a pasture with trees, finally making its way straight toward our house. Along that road my daddy, his wagon, and the surprise must travel before sundown that day, and I strained my eyes up and down the road as the afternoon waned and shadows grew long. Then at last a slowly-moving speck appeared on the road, grew bigger than a man's hand, disappeared behind the pasture, and then became a wagon and mules plodding along the road toward our yard, my daddy sitting up in front of the wagon on a board seat, wearing his broad black hat like a stagecoach bandit.

The Western Auto in Hubbard had wrapped the tricycle in butcher's paper, a mystery object for a barefooted five-year-old in Dickies overalls. Out from the paper came the grandest firetruck-red tricycle decorated with white spokes in the wheels, black rubber grips on the handlebars, and a ribbed foot rest along the axle behind the rider's saddle.

When I sat on the rider's seat, my bare feet rested comfortably on the rubber pedals at the center of the big front wheel. I soon found I could pedal easily, and except for a few problems in turning in tight circles, occasioning the cycle to stub the front wheel and throw me over the cool handlebars, I was soon pedaling up and down the length of the front porch, the trike's humming wheels making a pleasurably dangerous sound as I hummed over the uneven boards. Luckily for me, my parents quickly tired of this spectacle and retired inside the house, thus giving me the freedom to speed, throw on the brakes, and fall over. It may be that only children understand the principle of harmonizing vulgar sound effects with racket. Probably it was in my nature at that age to blend crude, wet mouth noises and the clatter of the tricycle's wheels into a sound track for my free-wheeling sport. Engine mimicry loaded with r-r-r-r-r-r-r satisfied for a while, but when Dick Tracy appeared on the scene a siren was added: r-r-r-r-r-e-e-e-e-e-r-r-r-e-e-e. Mingling vowels and consonants asked for a concentration that caused me to neglect the skill needed to make wide turns at the far, higher end of the porch, and I stubbed the front wheel and threw the machine and me off the end of the porch.

"I knew you'd break your neck first thing," said Momma, hurrying to aid her bawling child. Actually, my neck was fine, and a couple of scrapes on my elbows were nothing to cry about, but several nicks in the tricycle's red paint job were worth the crying and screaming.

My dad came and put the trike back on the porch.

"I don't think it's damaged much," he said, "These handlebars are still straight, and no wheels are twisted. Just a bit of paint's gone, that's all. I'd say ride in the yard, not up on the porch. It's safer that way. You can't ride over the edge of the yard."

"I didn't think he was big enough for a tricycle, but you were bound and determined to get him one. Now, see, he nearly killed hisself," she said.

"Well, I don't see it was a death-defying leap, Jane," said Daddy. "Most kids run off the porch now and again."

In such cases as the red tricycle episode my daddy proved himself a calm and reasoning man, and yet I know virtually nothing about his political notions, nothing about his thoughts on the economic or political lot of people like himself. What, for example, did he think of President Roosevelt's policy on cotton in 1934 when farmers were asked to plow under a percentage of their cotton crop in order to jack up prices? I find no evidence in his accounts book of that policy affecting his or Mr. David's planting of their mutual crops, though I do know that at some point in those years they were asked to shoot and dispose of cattle for similar reasons as those for destroying cotton. There was a gully near the big red barn where my cousin Melvin Junior and I in later years terrorized ourselves by digging up moldy cow bones and skulls, naked and bleached after years of being underground, where the dead cattle had been thrown after being shot.

A single anecdote from memory speaks to me about Daddy's political awareness. On the occasion of President Franklin Roosevelt's State of the Union address in January, 1938, my father asked me to go with him to a neighbor's house to "hear Mr. Roosevelt talk on the radio." I was proud to go, even though going on a walk with Daddy was more strenuous than walking with my mother. If she and I visited a neighbor and I tired from lack of anything to do except listen, and if I whined on the return trip, she would lug me part of the way on her back. My dad made me walk.

The neighbor lived across the creek and beyond a spacious field, so I walked and trotted alongside Daddy. He helped me cross the creek and climb through a barbed wire fence on the other side. Because it was cold weather, we hiked over frosty rows of fallen corn stalks, then we came to the house of the neighbor who owned a radio. I recall it being the dark of winter inside the living room where a cathedral radio sat on a table and a fire burned in a fireplace. I'm sure I gaped around like an open pitcher during the time we were there, for the man of the house was a diabetic, and he had one leg amputated. Never before had I seen a person with only one leg, and I was hypnotized by the sight of an elderly gentleman seated in a rocking chair, one foot rowing the chair, a stump of a leg going along for the ride. So there we set, our backs to the fire, a one-legged man, a Depression farmer with a walrus mustache, and a jug-eared kid with his mouth ajar, looking at the radio and listening to that posh Roosevelt voice reassuring us that our government cared about us.

My daddy must have thought the President was talking to him in that State of the Union, for Mr. Roosevelt noted that one-third of Americans worked on farms and that a vast number of them lived in poverty. The President was anxious to assist these farm workers, and he outlined three potential remedies for their plight. The first option must have sounded ironic to my hard-working parent: cut the costs of farm labor. However, Mr. Roosevelt said this option was unthinkable, as it would re-invent human slavery. In the second choice, government would become a guarantor of farm prices and undercut the excess of farm production. Not possible, he said, without ruining the country's economy. My dad may have thought it was ruined already where he lived. Finally, Mr. Roosevelt suggested that farmers themselves must accept responsible farming practices which maintained reasonable supplies of produce and thus assured adequate prices through supply and demand. This final option, he went on, was central to a program for balanced agriculture presently before both houses of Congress. Whether my daddy worried much about supply and demand beyond his corn crib and my mother's kitchen, I have no way of knowing. But I think I know how he must have felt about Mr. Roosevelt's acknowledgment that some forces in the country wanted to insure cheap labor in order to encourage industry. The President's voice went on in a strong and encouraging manner, drifting out of that church-shaped radio, a soft electric light hiding its bulb somewhere in its insides.

Doubtless my daddy discussed the President's words with me on the way home, but all I recall is my own attempt to uncover the mysteries of a one-legged man. Where did the leg go? Did he bury it in the ground? And did it feel anything? Would it come back and call out to its owner in a ghostly voice like those disembodied limbs in the stories my sisters told me in the dark? One thing I'm sure about is that I walked all the way back home.

Although my daddy still called me Baby, his behavior with me seemed to hint at a theory about growing boys that escaped my mother's attention. Thus, it was probably good that it was he and not my mother who discovered me lively engaging in my first sexual experiment in my fifth year. The object of my passion was a living doll; well, literally a doll. This doll had porcelain arms and legs as well as a similar ceramic head, its cheeks and lips glazed with a crimson blush. Dark, glossy hair with a glasslike finish waved about her head and gave the doll features resembling the cute and daring flappers you'd see in nineteen-thirties' magazines. Maybe that was where I'd picked up my saucy ideas; otherwise, I'd had naught for sex education.

All I remember is that a fantasy about what lay underneath the doll's lacy, blue dress had bloomed in my young mind. One day, then, Momma had gone on a solo visit to a neighbor woman and left me in the care of my daddy who pretty much left me to my own devices. It was while I was giving the doll a ride on my scooter, cruising her among the white chickens, that I had the big idea: I could take her under the porch and explore her body. One end of the porch, the one I'd soon ride off with a red tricycle, was high enough off the ground that underneath it provided a cave-like playground, a secret hideaway where I often retired with bricks, bottles, and tiny cars. On this day I retired there with the porcelain doll in the blue dress and in a mysterious state of agitation, I lifted the lace and found a smooth cloth tummy with no distinguishing gender features. However, the notion struck me that thrills galore of some mystifying nature would occur if I were as unclothed as the dollie. It was my misfortune that my mother sometimes dressed me in a set of striped coveralls, a type of union suit which was a single garment sporting metal snaps down the front. It was easy getting those snaps undone. Soon I was as bare as my doll lady.

The specifics of my racy examinations are lost to history. But the emotional distress which came with my discovery that I couldn't get back inside the coveralls is still a part of my memory. When my dad came looking for me and looked underneath the porch, he found his five-year-old son with a porcelain doll, struggling to get his behind back into a pair of wrong-side-out coveralls. Daddy's comments are also lost to history, but I recall no punishment, which includes no telling on me to my mother.

Chapter 3

WHAT ALL I LEARNED IN FIRST GRADE

I began first grade at the age of six in a number-three, tin washtub. Make all the jokes you want about tubs with handles on the sides and lye soap and the bathing habits of country people on Saturday night, but my weekly bath in my mother's laundry tub was a sober ritual. My mother heated pans of water on the kitchen stove and dashed the tub half full so I'd not overflow onto the linoleum, and my sister Lucy scrubbed my sudsy hair into peaks with homemade soap, ivory-tinted pyramids of lye and pork rinds that looked appetizingly like peanut-butter fudge. But the ritual became its most serious of all one Saturday evening when my sister Lucy raised up from the tub, pointed one dripping finger at my pale body soaking in the water and spoke fateful words to my mother.

"Start him in first grade this fall, and I'll repeat a year to keep an eye on him."

Momma eased some dirty plates into a pan on the kitchen table, and pulled a flour-sacking towel off the stove and dried dish suds from her hands and came and looked down at me in the tub. I didn't know what was going on.

"He's so little," Momma said. "Maybe we'd best wait another year before sending him off to school. He'd be afraid, wouldn't he?" She fretted her hands with the towel. "Big kids can be so full of meanness."

Suddenly in our cheerful kitchen, familiar chairs, ice-box, and pots and pans collected all around like a family, a risk-free discussion of school took on an ominous aspect. Up to then most of the talk between my mother and my sister had been a background musical, its rhythm cheerful, intimate, and comforting in a setting where a single coal-oil lamp on the kitchen table gave soft light that allowed shadows behind the cookstove and pantry.

"You'all can't send me to school until I'm big and mean, too," I declared from the tub. However, my sister asserted that I was already mean, and reasoned that I would grow into big over the course of the year. Lucy was volunteering to be my guide and champion during my first year by repeating the eleventh grade, the final year required under Texas law in 1938, and which she had completed.

"Maybe he'd be starting a year early, but he's ready as a pup," she said. "He knows his ABCs when he wants to, and draws birdhouses and colors inside the lines." She dug a wash cloth into my ears looking for dirt. "Besides, I'll thrash any kids that tease him about his big ears."

"Momma! Lute's being mean about my ears!" I splashed some water on the floor to get attention. "It hurts, too!"

"Aw, she's just teasing you, Baby. Don't you want to be a big boy and go to school?"

"No, I'm little, and big kids will hit me with rocks, and bricks, and iron things. Why can't I just play under the porch? You can bring me tea-cakes and Ovaltine." I didn't have to be a big kid to understand that my peaceful days underneath the front porch were numbered.

"Climb out of the tub and dry off before you make the Mississippi float us all the way to Fort Worth." Lucy covered me in a big, white towel. "When you get your Mickey Mouse pajamas on, I'll tell you about school. You never saw so many swings and see-saws and picture books in your life." She looped my Mickey Mouse buttons and patted my hair. "I'll betcha a nickel nobody ever told you how much fun recess is."

And on such wise was my introduction to first grade at Cottonwood Country School. Six years as a solitary, leisured knock-about, spoiled by the attentions of females, had left me totally unprepared for a wider, wilder society, that lower class inhabited by rowdies, bullies, "regular" boys, and "saucy" girls.

Cottonwood, everyone in Hill County called it. As in: "He goes to school at Cottonwood, but his mother walks him part way every morning until he stops crying." So, yes, I cried every morning during my first weeks of first grade, cried at breakfast, cried on the porch, cried walking down the road.

Of course, my mother rigged me out each morning with the care of an old-time sailor putting his sails in order to catch the wind. She'd make sure my face was shiny, take a brush and slick down my hair, check the shoulder straps of my overalls to see they were not twisted, and stow my sack lunch down in my book satchel. She'd made the book satchel herself, cutting and sewing cotton-sacking into a pouch that hung off my shoulder with a strap. There was even a denim flap to overhang the mouth of the satchel and protect my writing tablets and Crayolas. To be sure I'd not lose my satchel, my mother wrote my name on it with a purple indelible pencil.

"You be careful and don't get in no accidents," my mother cautioned me each morning. "I'll worry about you all day, Baby, if you get hurt." She would sniffle and push her red hair from her forehead, then wipe her eyes, imagining me being taken to the doctor with varied broken limbs. For my sister she also had words of advice. "Don't let him bite off more than he can chew. You know how he is."

After Lucy and I got out of the yard, my mother would come out to the road and wave at us until we were out of sight. Those mornings were my first exercises in pulling away from my mother who had been as protective of me for six years as Mother Goose. Of course, it was not as if the school lay just around the corner.

Four or five country miles of fields, pastures, gullies, bob-wire fences, and muddy creeks separated my house from Cottonwood School, and chances of being gored by a bull, set upon by a coachwhip snake, or drowned upside down in creek water were equal possibilities. Since the Hickman Ranch provided a setting for these colorful adventures, my champion and guide, Lucy, and sometimes my mother, escorted me for the first mile along the wagon road which led past danger-free zones like my mother's garden where she'd take a salt-cellar to dust tomatoes she'd eat right off the vine. But after about a mile we'd leave the road as it went on toward the big red barn, and Lucy and I'd tuck underneath the strands of a bob-wire fence and make our own paths across open country.

On one of these early first-grade adventure hikes, I dawdled in a sandy patch with a feisty and spiky hornytoad I'd caught, holding him up by his tail and poking his horns to see if he'd spit in my eye like I'd heard. But I'd failed to notice he was parked in a bed of red ants. By the time my sister got to me I was swarmed with red ants, their stings trailing up my legs all the way to my belly button.

"Lord have mercy, Leon, you got red ants all up and down yourself," said my not-quite-so-observant bodyguard. "I thought you were having the St. Vitus dance."

Lucy pulled my overalls off, shook them out and put me back in them, and returned my yelling, crying self to my mother. Red ants were just part of my continuing education. On the whole, however, I was neither absent nor tardy that first year. After a while even my mother stopped crying while she made smashed-banana sandwiches and sacked my lunch.

After Lucy and I crossed over Cottonwood Creek, we could see the white schoolhouse just beyond the dirt road which older people called "The Pike," and on the East side of the old Cottonwood cemetery with its wooden crosses and granite angels. One morning Lucy stopped beside the road and waited for me, who she called "the ten o'clock scholar," to catch up to her, and pointed toward the cemetery. She had a history lesson for me.

"Leon, you see over there at the cemetery?"

"I can see," I said, "What do you want?"

"You can't see it now, 'cause it's gone. But there used to be a store there, and you'd buy axe handles and cotton sacks and milk buckets in there good as you please."

"Can you buy Butterfingers in there?" The history lesson was starting to interest me.

"No, silly, not now, but used to be. That store belonged to Old Man Mose. And he had a mule barn there, and you could buy a mule, or trade one off if you didn't like it."

"I'd trade off my mule for a bee-bee-gun," I said.

"If we don't get you to school, you won't have any more sense than that mule," my sister said.

The school itself was a long frame building with lots of windows to yield warm, Texas sunlight into the classrooms. Old photos I now own show nine large panes in each window and a wire mesh to keep out flies if the windows were raised. A long porch like a verandah was reached by several wooden steps, then big doors opened into the foyer of the schoolhouse. Passing straight through the entrance way took one into an auditorium where each school day began with ceremonies performed to wake up mostly farm kids to their allegiance to Old Glory and their obligations to be clean and brush their teeth, but mostly just to wake them up. I usually managed to stand near my sister throughout the group singing of rhyming words out of funny-smelling songbooks, but my comfort level went down like a lost chord during the principal's prayer. I knew the next order of business was to march off in the wake of our teachers to whatever doom awaited us in our classrooms. In my case doom awaited, I knew, in the persons of Miss La Moine Shull, my teacher, and Kenney Dorvall, my evil nemesis.

"Lute," I'd whine to my sister, "I don't feel good. I think I have a fever. You guess I might need to go home and let Momma take a look at me? Maybe I need a doctor?"

My sister had heard these whines before, but she'd feel my forehead and pronounce me to be fit for going to class. Several of Lucy's teenage friends would look at me and stick out their tongues and point their fingers at me and try to shame me.

There must have been a trillion classrooms all over the world that looked just like my first-grade classroom: rows of small desks attached to cast-iron legs bolted to the floor so as not to wobble like the kids sitting in them; a great black slab of chalkboard extending along one wall, a line of carefully printed ABCs in colored chalk marching along the top; the teacher's fine desk of deal standing at the head of the room, a vase of fresh flowers at one corner; charts along one wall for collecting gold stars if pupils brushed their teeth, held up their hands before going to the toilet, and knew the words for Dick, Jane, Baby, and Spot; and several big windows that afforded views of the playground's swings and seesaws.

The exotically-named Miss La Moine Shull was the first "other woman" in my life. The only women playing supporting roles in my first six years had been either family or near-family: sisters, cousins, aunts, neighbors of my mother. Now here was this woman who exhibited as much authority as my mother, spent as much time with me as my sister, and combined the lure and risk of Eve. Indeed, Miss Shull was prettier than any female I'd ever seen up close. There was a suggestion of the movie star about her, a hint of Loretta Young with dark hair and an extra ten pounds. She parted her hair in the middle and styled it with curlers, and plucked her eyebrows, and painted her lips into a red heart. A sunny, cheerful disposition would have been anyone's first impression of my teacher, but they would have been wrong if they expected the disposition to follow her through the door into her classroom. Regardless of how attractive and pleasant Miss Scull may have appeared at a picnic for parents, her muscular, no-nonsense attitude in the classroom intimidated this six-year-old kid with big ears who had been hi-jacked onto his first-grade adventure.

Without a doubt I was the meekest child among Miss Shull's flock of country urchins. My yellowing photo of Cottonwood's pupils and teachers, taken the year I was in first grade, displays a gallery of unblinking scholars gazing into an unseen camera in mid-day; there are forty-two pupils, first-graders and second-graders down front, mature eleventh-graders standing in back. Three girls are grinning broadly, two are smiling, boys either scowl or look pained. I am in the third row, totally bewildered, the smallest kid jammed between two upper-grade pupils as if I were there on second thought.

And yet for all my timidity, Miss Shull and I had words over the numeral eight. I stayed at my desk and copied the alphabet in my Indian-head tablet with my cedar pencil, and I colored within the lines. As far as reciting from our little readers, I was up to the mark. I recognized "cat," "dog," "Daddy," and "Mother" when she called me up to the chair beside her desk and asked me to read from the book. I was quiet and did not beat a path to the pencil sharpener. And yet we had a definite fight over the correct way to write the numeral eight on the chalkboard. I admit I had the numeral seven backwards for a while, but Miss Shull's guiding hand corrected my seven without any backtalk from me. But I couldn't see why the eight was not drawn with one O above another O. Like a snowman. Miss Shull, however, believed strongly in the eight drawn with a single wraparound swoop that looked like an electric-train track, and she demanded compliance. I resisted and hid my double-0s behind my hand when it was my time at the chalkboard. But Miss Shull saw the glorious fulfillment of her entire teaching career resting on training my hand to make her version of the eight; thus, she introduced the ruler from her desk drawer as the final arbitrator of our debate. I compromised.

I suspect Miss Shull saw her class of farmyard escapees as a Peaceable Kingdom, where the lamb and the lion kicked back side by side and shared their deviled ham and home-canned peaches at recess and lunch. Only such a state of mind could explain her decision to position me in a desk immediately in front of that occupied by Kenney Dorvall. Kenney recognized a victim as soon as a mother's boy blundered onto his patch, which included his desk and any contingent desks, the front porch, the schoolyard, the play equipment, and the boys' toilets, maybe the cosmos.

Nothing in Kenney's appearance marked him as a bully. No busted up nose. No tattoos of anchors on his biceps. No penitentiary stripes. He was chunkier than I, a year older, and he had blond hair and freckles like a cherub. In light of my subsequent experiences during grade school, I realize that he and I may have been equally to blame for his bullying. I looked so much like a victim, what could he do? Somebody had to pick on me. He was it.

I'd noticed right away that Kenney always placed a mechanical pencil in the little groove at the top of his desk. I had to put a "cedar pencil," a thin rod of graphite passing through a round stick of cedar, in the groove in my desk. These pencils were cheap, and they smelled like a cedar chest. Not fun to draw or write with. In contrast, that mechanical pencil had a little eraser in its top, and a metallic barrel that wound lead out of the tip when you twisted it. Best of all, there was a shiny clip below the eraser that you could use to fasten the pencil into your shirt pocket. As far as I could tell, that pencil represented the ultimate in writing equipment in the year 1938. Boy, I wanted it.

When Miss Shull made us practice making letters of the alphabet on our lined newsprint tablets, I'd peek back at Kenney and admire the ease of his writing with that grand mechanical pencil.

One morning Miss Shull sat at her desk helping a first-grader read about Dick and Jane. I felt a light punch in my back and looked around to find Kenney putting a finger to his lips and offering me the mechanical pencil.

"Betcha you'd write good with this pencil," he whispered. Oh, what joy I felt! I was going to hold the magic pencil!

I took the pencil. It was a blue one, and its beveled lines were "modern" without me being aware of it. I just knew that holding it made me look grownup. I began to scribble on my tablet, but I got no letters, only scratches on my paper. I was puzzled. Where was the magic writing?

I felt another punch in my back, and looked around to see Kenney covering his mouth with his hand, smothering giggles.

"What's the matter with it?" I guiltily checked out the teacher to be sure she was busy.

"April's fool!" whispered Kenney. "Which one of the dwarfs are you? Dopey, or Sleepy? Can't you see it ain't got no lead in it?" He was heaving, red in the face to keep from laughing. I looked at the end of the pencil and saw only a metal tip sticking out. No lead.

"You want to swap for it? Whatcha gimmie?"

Here was an offer I'd never dreamed of, a prospect for ownership of the grandest writing instrument in the world. And it never entered my mind that the pencil might be out of lead, even busted. Probably wouldn't matter very much if you could still clip it into your pocket.

Miss Shull was still busy with Dick and Jane. Good. There was opportunity for barter. I'd learned enough about swaps and trades from my sister so I could make an offer.

"Can I take it home today and bring you something good tomorrow?" I watched Kenney with one eye, Miss Shull with the other. Kenney leaned forward and pinched my arm, a real stinger. He seemed oblivious to any threat from the teacher.

"Sure, Dopey, but if you don't bring me something I like, I'm going to come to your house tomorrow night and cut your throat while you're asleep." He dragged a finger across his neck and made my flesh crawl.

I know my mother couldn't make sense of the hurly-burly of her son that evening as I searched desperately among my limited possessions for something to trade for the pencil and for my life. Images of Kenney and his knife floated in and out of my consciousness and made me extremely nervous. And my wealth of enviable goods was, I admitted, quite limited, consisting of several comic books, three or four metal cars, a rubber ball, a tin sheriff's badge, a toy watch on a chain, and a book of cut-outs for paper dolls. I didn't think Kenney would go crazy about the paper dolls, and the rubber ball really belonged to another boy from whom I'd stolen it. I could only guess what kind of things would satisfy my seatmate, whom I had to admit seemed much more advanced in the things of the world than I was.

Finally I checked into my collection of marbles, my most prized possessions. I kept them in a Bull Durham tobacco sack, which pulled closed at the top with yellow string. From the sack I poured a handful. There were solid reds and blues, some large clear glass ones with golden swirls inside, and one or two old-fashioned crock marbles my sister had given me. I found a Colgate toothpaste box and stuffed it to the limit with marbles. I figured if I loved the marbles so much, they would also be prized by Kenney. Though I hated to lose my glass marbles, there was the matter of getting my throat cut if the deal went bad.

There he was the next morning, standing at the top of the steps, positioned on the edge of the porch like a bulldog waiting for the mailman. Kenney wore the same blue-and-white stripy overalls that I did; fittingly, we both displayed a bird of prey, a hawk, in a red diamond on the breast pocket of our overalls. Some boys like my buddy Royce Dillard wore blue overalls, and their diamond patches for some odd reason showed a kangaroo. Thinking back, I realize our mothers picked out and bought our overalls at the same clothing store, Mr. Towbolowsky's dry-goods store in Hubbard. Those new overalls, the best my mother's egg money could buy, went a long way toward making me look well-turned-out by Momma each morning. Eggs equals overalls was a formula she used to give her son the look of quality.

Kenney had also received the same tooth-comb inspection at the hands of his mother. He was clean, neat, scrubbed, in his own presentation a vision of some fallen angel. The big difference between him and me was that he knew how to wrap four fingers around his thumb and make a fist into a perfect supporting instrument for his role on the school ground.

"Whatcha got for me, Dopey?"

I took my loaded family-size Colgate box from my satchel and handed it up to Kenney on the top step, hoping the weight and size of it would distract attention from my lack of both those qualities.

"Rattle it back and forth," I said. "Guess what's in it."

Kenney shook the red and white box, and it sounded like a box of rocks.

"Rocks," said Kenney, just before one end popped open and marbles erupted from the box and peppered onto the porch, bouncing, pinging, and rolling every which way. Glass-eyed marbles swept along the porch; some tumbled off the porch, and rattled down the steps and leapt into the dirt at my feet. Up on the porch kids chased marbles and dropped to their knees to gobble them up. I looked down at two glass marbles and one crock marble coming to rest near my foot, and I could not have felt more doomed if they had been three cannon balls lofted at me from a dark wood. My deal for the mechanical pencil was going bust right in front of my eyes, while the thought crossed my mind that I'd never be safe at night anymore.

I dared to raise my eyes to the porch, and I saw Kenney standing in a tangle of first-and-second graders, a mob of wild kids, some yet on their knees, scrambling after loose marbles. One or two were holding up rescued marbles in their hands as if they were prizes for something. But Kenney held my attention. He was red in the face, the neat part in his combed hair had come undone so a tuft of hair fell over one eye, and he was punching the air with one fist, four fingers wrapped around a thumb, while waving around his other hand, still holding the empty Colgate box. And he was screaming.

"My marbles! Them's my marbles! Everybody's stealing my marbles!"

I could believe my eyes. I'd become used to imagining Kenney turning into a monster. But I couldn't believe my ears, because he was acting like the marbles belonged to him, as if the spilled contents of the toothpaste carton were his, and everybody had to give them back. Could it be that Kenney liked the marbles, and our swap was a success and my life had been saved?

From near my foot I picked up three marbles and walked up the steps. Other kids were handing marbles to Kenney, and he was dropping them into the Colgate box. I gave him the ones I'd picked up and watched him drop them into the box with the others.

"Nine, ten, eleven," he counted. "You think I got all of 'em?"

"If the box is full," I said.

A few minutes after I scooted into my seat and arranged my mechanical pencil in the slot on my desk, I felt a punch in my back. Miss Shull was standing in the door of our room talking to another teacher, so I looked around to see Kenney shushing me with a finger across his mouth. He talked like a ventriloquist without moving his lips.

"That's a crackerjack swap we made, Dopey." He winked one eye. "I like marbles. Maybe me and you can play 'keeps' sometimes. Then I'll win your cat-eyes." After checking on the teacher, he went on. "You got any steel ballies?"

"Maybe," I said. I was certain of one thing, though. I didn't have a clue as to what he was talking about, because I didn't know a "cat-eye" from a "steel ballie." But I didn't want to break up this new truce with Kenney, which seemed to be founded on a commercial venture. If he wanted to play a game called "keeps," I'd be willing. All I had to do was ask my sister to explain these new developments.

I like to fantasize that one day Miss La Moine Shull took a Greyhound bus from Cottonwood to Hollywood and co-starred with Clark Gable as a glamorous film star and changed her name to Claudette Colbert; however, when I get real I suspect the bus dropped her each Texas summer on a small college campus where she spent hot days in a library, working to earn additional credits toward her teaching certification. Maybe she reached the heights of elementary school principal. Of course, I have no factual history for her. But one thing I know for certain: Miss Shull's image exists in my memory, imprinted there in my sixth and seventh years, as a goddess of our school-room and playground, at one time creating awe and dread, at another time security, while she maintains in my adult consciousness as an icon of the love and influence that's so critical in transforming kids from poor families into young people with futures. In my case, she put books into my hands and turned up the fire under my latent imagination; she armed this country kid with a means for defeating or, sometimes, escaping from distressing situations when life acted up. But I still watch for her at the movies.

My first reader in the first grade was, unsurprisingly, the classic tale of Dick, Jane, Father, Mother, Baby, and Spot. I can't recall being perplexed with style, diction, characterization, plot, or symbolism in the text. Therefore, I fell into a habit that followed me through countless future classes: reading a book during down-times. Miss Shull placed stacks of little books around the room which we could choose to read on our own after we'd completed her required projects, and I fell in love with the pictures and stories I'd find during those quiet periods. I can recall the first book I ever read all the way through on my own. It told about a little Indian boy who had no name at the beginning of the story, because the custom of his tribe was to give children names based on some animal or bird. If a child pointed to a bear and called it "bear," he or she became known by some quality of the animal. But the little Indian boy in the story was causing his mother and daddy some anxiety, for though he was growing up he had never spoken a word. On the last page of the book there was a painting of a cardinal in a tree, and the little boy pointed at the bird and said, "Red bird." His mother and daddy happily named him "Little Red Bird," an act that made me happy with the parents and led me to beg my mother to call me "Little Red Bird."

Like any six-year-old country kid hi-jacked by school wardens, however, I found recess to be the maximum spellbinder of each day. One of the friends I'd made was a shy boy named Royce who, like me, behaved in class and acted so bashful that he competed with me for class waif. He was probably near my age, small in size, but had more freckles across his nose. He always wore blue overalls. When recess arrived, Royce and I joined in playground activity, which I seem to recall consisted of dashing wildly around and over everything as if our energies had been dammed up for hours and we'd bust if the dam didn't. But Kenny remained my major first-grade influence after Miss Shull.

With the passing of time, he and I returned to our "business" enterprises, and we both lost a batch of topnotch marbles one day when Miss Shull found us behind the school house playing "keeps" in a sandy patch and confiscated our "cat eyes" and "steel ballies." As soon as she spotted us down on our knees, excitedly knuckling marbles over a circle we'd drawn in the dirt, she knew we were playing the forbidden game of "keeps." When she appeared around the corner of the school house, our teacher looked like an avenging angel. She said "keeps" was too much like gambling.

When the end of the school year arrived on 18 May 1939, Miss Shull thought enough of me to give me a major role in the "Closing Program of Cottonwood School." My friend Royce was at the top of the program, going out on stage in the auditorium wearing his serious face, and reciting a piece titled "The Report Card." I followed Royce with my part. I'd had to memorize a poem with the title "Where's My Dog?" which required me to walk out in front of our families, them all dressed up in their finest go-to-meeting clothes, and--the hard part--*act out* my little play. My poem actually carried stage and acting directions, which I'd had to memorize. It began: "Small boy enters. He has been crying and is wiping his eyes on his sleeve." Then I launched into my speech: "Say, have any of you folks seen my dog? He's mostly black and yellow. His name is Beauty, and he is the cutest little fellow." The role was most demanding in the places where I'd pick out some person in the audience, look directly at them, and speak my lines, like "Say, lady, have you seen a dog?"

My performance was followed by a third piece of drama titled "Dolly Has the Flu," which featured Kenney, appropriately, as "the Doctor." The female lead was dark-haired Dixie Lynn, playing "the Distressed Mother."

At the time, I wasn't convinced the role Miss Shull chose for me was a prize, because I'd put in a lot of rehearsal at home under the direction of my sister. In later years, however, I was proud I'd been chosen to do it, because Daddy was in the audience to see his first-grader up on the stage. There he was out there where I could see him, sitting with my anxious mother, dressed in a dark coat, wearing shined black brogans, and holding his large black hat on his lap. Though my mother had trimmed his wild mustache, he still looked like an outlaw escaped from the latest Gene Autry "Western." Of course, my dad still thought of me as his "baby," for he couldn't have known about my loss of innocence during this first year of school with the help of my worldly-wise friend, Kenney. I'm sure my promotion to second grade, therefore, was deserved and reflected my new sophistication. Daddy was gone by the time our next Christmas holiday rolled around, and the lives of my mother and my sister and myself were interrupted and changed forever.

Chapter 4

BE A GOOD BOY

It was in the summer after my seventh birthday that the squadrons of Luftwaffe bombers began to float into my dreams. The planes were enormous and sinister as they hovered between the clouds and the full moon, their shadows like giant birds moving along the earth. From beneath their wings fell bombs resembling cannonballs, and they streamed to the earth and hit and bounced and exploded in flames. In the dream I struggled to escape from the bombs as they burst in our front yard, but could only stumble in slow motion among my mother's geraniums and hollyhocks and sunflowers. I'd awaken from the nightmare to find myself struggling among the bedclothes, and my mother at my bedside reassuring me I was safe in my own bed. After numerous episodes of me thrashing my pillow and crying out bloody-murder, my mother brought the matter before the breakfast table one morning while she "waited on us hand and foot," as she called it.

"Leon's having his scary dreams again." Brushing her red hair back from her forehead with one hand, holding out a coffee pot with the other, she looked at my daddy and my grandfather. Daddy was stirring a heaping spoonful of rich cow's cream into his Grape Nuts Bran cereal. I couldn't imagine how he'd keep it out of his big mustache. My grandfather was wiping a homemade biscuit into some milk gravy. They both stopped eating and stared across the table at me as if I'd just appeared out of nowhere.

"Well, Baby, tell us what-all scary things you saw in your dream." Daddy smiled at me. "It'll be no bother to us now. Why, we'll beat the living daylights out of those scary things, won't we?" Behind his smile, my dad in his big mustache looked mean enough himself to do it alright.

"Lucy said don't never tell a dream before breakfast so it won't come true," I said. I sure didn't want those bombers showing up right after breakfast the minute I told on them.

"I expect your sister's right," said Daddy. "But that's if you tell the whole dream. Now there ain't a thing wrong with you just saying what-all it's about."

Momma set a bowl of her hot coffee in front of me, and I began to pinch up a soft biscuit into the coffee. When I'd pour thick cow's cream over the soaking biscuits, I'd have my usual breakfast. Everybody seemed to be watching me this morning, expecting me to tell about my scary dream. My cream melted in the coffee, made it rich looking.

"I didn't want to stomp all over Momma's hollyhocks," I said.

"Goodness gracious, Baby, you can't hurt your momma's flowers in a dream," said my mother. She placed a sugar bowl in front of me and paused to brush her hand through my hair, making it lay down around my ears. "Why, old flowers in the front yard don't amount to a hill of beans, nohow. Whatever made you think you'd stomp on them?"

The last night's vision of the terrible bombers and their unleashed firestorm was yet vivid and undiminished in my mind, as clear as the face of Shirley Temple on the bottom of my blue cereal bowl.

"Bombs," I said. Now they all stopped eating again. Even my grandfather quit sopping his gravy.

"I ain't never heard of nobody bombing some damn old hollyhocks," he said.

My daddy rested his spoon in his empty cereal bowl and passed it to my mother, and his face took on a worried look. He called my mother back from the wash pan, she drying her hands.

"Probably you ought'en let him run off to the Lees place so much. I know he plays a lot with their boy. But those folks are well-off enough to have a battery radio, and I'm a mind it's so much worldly things comes over it he's too young to hear."

When my mother came back from putting the dirty bowls and plates in her wash pan, she sat down on the bench near me and placed a hand on my shoulder and untwisted an overall strap I'd buckled in a hurry. She could tell I'd told as much of my dream as my daddy and grandfather were likely to hear, and she addressed them with some irritation in her voice, like as if her red hair were putting her up to it.

"What I think is you'all'd best stop talking about that old Hitler mess at the supper table. He hears you'all telling about that war over across the water, and then he goes and has these scary dreams about it."

Daddy and my grandfather looked at her now instead of me. I could tell they thought she was blaming them for my scary dreams, and I guessed she was pretty much in the right. But part of the blame rested on me, too, because I was drawn to their talk about a coming war over across the water. In the evenings after supper I'd sit on a bench and prop my elbows on the table and lean into the light made by our coal-oil lamp, and I'd soak up the rambling conversation between my dad and my grandfather, names of far-off places and distant people. Germany. England. France. I'd sneak my fingers into my ears, and I'd take them out. Sometimes they'd just talk about cows getting out of a pasture or the Johnson grass taking over the cotton; but, again, they'd trade news somebody'd told them about the carryings-on over across the waters.

"I'm thinking, Mr. Waller," Daddy would say, pulling off his work shoes and tucking them underneath his chair, "we ought to stretch some bobwire across the shallow end of that tank by the meadow. Soon as the water level goes down in July, we'll get some young calves adventuring out there, and we'll waste a morning pulling them out of the mud."

"Sure as hell," agreed my grandfather. "They ain't got the sense to stay up on the bank. It'll be like it was in the tank up by the red barn the day we pulled several out with the mules." My grandfather picked up a used Arbuckle coffee can, spat snuff juice into it, and set it down beside his chair and went on talking. "I heard one of them Morgan boys might get called up by the Army if this war don't get settled. Wonder what old man Morgan will do for help in the fields?"

I watched him spit in the can, hoping he'd get spit on the floor, because my mother would have to mop it up. I hoped she's fuss at him about it. I couldn't figure out why my daddy, who neither chewed tobacco nor used bad language, allowed my grandfather to do both. He wouldn't let me do stuff like that in the house.

My grandfather and Hitler drifted into my circle of attention at about the same time, and both of them caught me off guard at about the age of seven. And back then it might have been hard for me to tell you which one alarmed me more.

All I knew was one day my grandfather showed up out of nowhere to live with us. Because he had two daughters and a son other than my mother, he occasionally spent some time with each one, though he mainly drifted around nobody knew where. Some people in the family said he was a cowboy, and worked livestock in lean times. My mother had one photo of him dressed up in a cowboy hat and boots, his head thrown back, drinking something from a large clay jug with a spout, and if it was anything but water you couldn't have proved it by me. He was a small man, tucked into denim pants, who always wore a soft felt hat with a snap brim. He'd also grit his teeth and grind them and use bad language, so think Pretty Boy Floyd and you'll have a useful image of Mr. Waller. His positive first impression on me, a red herring if there ever was one, took place the day he told my mother he wanted to teach her how to use a gun.

Momma was sweeping our front yard with her kitchen broom, easing broken glass and pebbles and rusty nails into the flower beds where such booby traps wouldn't be stepped on when I went barefoot.

My grandfather stood on the porch, once in a while spitting tobacco juice into the yard below him. He and my mother were gossiping about her sisters, Sis and Ett, which led my mother to ask when he'd last visited them.

"Oh, I seen Sis probably a month back," he said. "She's got so many dadgum kids I can't get no rest when I'm there. The youngest one's only about a year old, squalls all the time."

My mother stopped sweeping and knocked the broom against the corner of the porch and handed it to me. I began making a road in the dirt with it.

"If you didn't come from Sis and Wylie's, where was you?"

"Been around, I guess," said my grandfather. "Don't make no difference."

"Well, that's what makes me worry about you," said my mother. "One day they'll find you in a ditch somewhere, the daylights beat out of you."

My grandfather came down the front steps into the yard. He put his hand inside his cotton sweater and dragged a gun from the waistband of his denims.

"You ever see a man with a Colt in his hand get the daylights beat out of hisself?"

He displayed the gun on his open palm. It was a revolver, both dark and shiny. The barrel looked long to me, a raised sight on the end. It had a criss-cross rubber grip, and you could see the trigger inside a metal circle underneath a cylinder with several holes peeking darkly at you like those in a wasp's nest. My grandfather twirled the cylinder with his thumb, and it made a buzzing sound that made me think of a June bug in a tree.

"Get that thing away from me," said my mother. "I know what guns do to people."

"A gun don't do nothing but what you want it to do," said my grandfather. "Ain't you ever pulled a trigger before?" He took the gun by its barrel and handed it toward my mother. "Here, let me show you how to hold it and you pull the trigger." He cocked the hammer back and placed the criss-crossed grip in her hands.

My mother gingerly took the revolver in both hands and pointed it off down toward the pasture beyond our yard fence. Her hands and the gun shook as if she were pointing a banty rooster at somebody instead of a Colt revolver. I got really scared seeing my mother holding a gun. Even in the cowboy picture shows I'd never seen a woman draw a gun and shoot anything.

Suddenly the gun roared and made a little cloud of smoke from the muzzle. My mother stepped backwards and looked surprised like she'd stepped on a baby chick. Nobody in their right minds could have guessed where that bullet went.

My grandfather bent over laughing and slapped his knees. When he straightened up, you could see tears in his eyes.

"Well, Bill," he said to my mother, "It'd be a lie if I said old Pretty Boy Floyd had to be scared of you!"

Besides the influence of the revolver, I'd never formed a bond with my grandfather. He was distant, never talked to me, displayed no grandfatherly gestures. One day he arrived back from a trip to town and brought a single large-sized, extra-big, yellow-papered Butterfinger candy bar, a miracle of milk chocolate and peanut-butter crisp, and gave it to my cousin Melvin Junior right in front of me. Thus began a prolonged out-in-the-daylight war between us that lasted for years, as I refused to ever call him Grandpa, only Mr. Waller, which Momma said was "disrespectful."

Skirmishes in the conflict were frequent. My grandfather would be livid every time I "told on him" to my mother about something he did "wrong," like sneaking the drinking dipper back into the water bucket without first rinsing it. Therefore, all open wounds being equal, it was not unexpected that morning when "Mr. Waller" allowed me and my big ears ought to be in bed after supper, anyways. I had no business in the kitchen when grown-ups brought up the Germans.

"Luther," he said to Daddy, "I always was told young'uns was supposed to be seen, not caterwauling about some Germans in the hollyhocks." For him, that settled it. "The damned Germans can't get over here noways."

It was during the summer after my first year at Cottonwood when we experienced the first alarms about my daddy's health. He had always shouldered the working load of good country people, even if he did look like a stagecoach bandit from the picture shows, a big, strong country man, seeming to take jubilant pride in clean fields, hardy cotton crops, and any day's work. There were minor symptoms now and then, however, to suggest he was not in his usual fine health, some discomfort in his chest and a general malaise. He was putting on weight, and I recall my mother began to chide him about "lopping Jersey cow cream all over them Grape Nuts." But the most ominous warning was his inability to keep pace with the field work. My mother was now more often seen in her bonnet following the wagons gathering corn from the fields, chopping heads of maize, and when the cotton rows needed weeding, she took a hoe and me to the fields. At first I took this going to work in the fields to be an adventure, one part fun, one part the romantic notion that I was now pretty much grown up to be permitted to work the cotton patch.

Troubled in mind by December, everyone waited for my daddy to have a fatal heart attack. The work in the fields, mostly which was getting in the remnants of the cotton crop, called "pulling bolls" because the bountiful seed cotton had already gone to the gin, was being done by my brother Arlo, helped in dribbles and spouts by Mr. Waller, my mother, my sister Lucy on weekends, my brother Marvin on stopovers from the wrestling circuit, and, of course, me.

Thus it was no surprise to anyone right after breakfast on the tenth day of December when my brother Marvin stepped up on the front porch carrying my father over his shoulders as a fireman might bring a victim from a building on fire.

"Oh, mercy, what's happened?" cried my mother, hurrying from the kitchen.

Marvin ducked his burden through the front door, and went to the big bed in the front room and rolled my father onto it. He positioned a pillow underneath his head and began to work off his shoes. The color was gone from my father's face.

"I thought he'd been gone to the closet a long time, so I went to check on him, and there he was, passed out right beside the toilet. I had to lift him over that darned fence."

My mother leaned over my father there, her face and voice grave, the nearest to passing out herself I'd ever seen.

"Daddy, you rest easy now," she said, trying at last to be calm for both of them. "Marvin's got you to the house, and we're calling Arlo and Mildred to go get Dr. Barnes." She turned to me, standing there with part of a biscuit still in my hands. "Go get your daddy's pills out of the safe in the kitchen. And bring some water."

When I got back with a glass I could hear Marvin out on the porch hollering for Arlo. We'd never had a telephone, which meant we always hollered across the fields at the neighbors' houses to get their attention, then we'd yell our messages to them. Marvin was hollering that Daddy was bad.

It was lucky for me that Lucy was staying with us that weekend, because nobody knew what to do with me in those hours of Daddy's dying. A pall-like climate spread itself from the first to the last in that front room of our house, usually a familiar place, but now something so unknowable for me had come to pass that if a literal cloud had factored into the room I'd not have been more mystified. Even my mother in her grief had become someone I didn't recognize. So in those hours when my father spent his last breaths, it was my sister who knew what to do with me. Lucy took my biscuit and directed me to the back room and helped me put my high-top shoes on.

"Daddy asked me to go round up Old Muley and her calf from the meadow and feed them in the lot," she said. "You want to help me?" She held my jacket in her hands, standing there.

"Okey-Doke, Lute," I said. Maybe if my daddy had that old cow on his mind, I thought, he'd be o.k.

Lucy and I walked up the road toward the red-haw trees, crossing over the fence there, and strode along the picked-over cotton rows in the direction of the meadow, looking for that old muley cow. It was a sunny, but chilly Sunday morning, the way a winter day in Texas can look lighted by sunshine, but still nip your nose with frost. I wore my coat, my gloves, and a leather cap with celluloid aviator's goggles you could pull down over your eyes if you pretended to be a fighter pilot like those in *Wings Comics*. Today I had my ear flaps snapped underneath my chin. My sister carried a short length of rope she'd brought from the cow lot.

"Momma's really crying in there where Daddy is," I said. "Will Daddy go up to Heaven while we're bringing Old Muley in, Lute?" Truth was, I didn't have much background about dying with which to compose a theory, except what I'd gathered from the engravings of winged angels and rays of sunlight diffused among clouds in Daddy's Big Old Bible. We didn't attend church, probably because we had no car, and hitching the mules and wagon, and riding to the nearest church at New Hope would consume most of Sunday, my parents' only day of rest.

"I don't know," she said, "but I guess if God wants him to."

We reached the meadow, and you could see frost melting off the prairie grass, the sun making ephemeral rainbow effects. Down by the fence line Old Muley patiently chewed her cud and watched us coming. The red and white calf stood near its mother, but acted spooked, its tail arched up, ready to kick up its heels and run.

"Lute, what's it like up there in Heaven?"

She stopped and studied the animals. We waited there. I didn't know if she was planning how to catch the momma cow or if she was making up an answer to my question. After a few minutes she took an ear of yellow corn from her pocket. It still had its shuck on.

"Old Muley'll come for the corn, and we'll get the rope on her, then she'll follow us down to the gate in the fence." Lucy held out the ear of corn and rattled its shuck. We watched Old Muley start to mosey in our direction. Her calf followed a few paces behind.

55

Lucy looked at me in my aviator cap and asked, "What do *you* think Heaven's like?"

I was stumped at first. What did I think? My only pictorial resources for a Heavenly Landscape were that Bible of Daddy's with the scary illustrations by Gustave Dore, and a blushing-orange hardbacked volume combining the books of the Apocrypha and the book of Revelations my father had received as a premium for buying several cans of Rosebud salve. As Old Muley ambled up and snuffed at the ear of corn, I flash-backed to my second-hand resources.

"Shoot, the best I can remember, Lute, is it's mostly angels. They wear white dresses, and long wings stick out of their backs like birds have." I had to think hard to recall the paintings I'd seen. "But I guess all the angels fly around in clouds and smoke, because the pictures I saw didn't have any cotton or tractors or cows. Just clouds and smoke." That didn't seem like much to go on, but it was all I could recall. "Do you think Heaven's really like in the pictures?"

Lucy slipped the rope over Old Muley's neck, and began to tug her in the direction of the gate. She was a gentle old whiteface cow, a good milker, one that my mother had virtually petted into a family member. The calf halfheartedly trotted alongside its mother.

"I expect you're pretty much right, little brother," said Lucy. "The only thing you left out is God."

My last image of my father while he lived: two pillows bent up against the iron-grille headboard of the bed on which he lay, his head reposing on them in the grace of tranquility. It was a lined face he presented, his forehead pale, not because of dying so much as because he had put his hat somewhere and couldn't find it. As it always was, my father's hair was brushed and tidy. Drops of water, probably from that I had brought in a glass from the kitchen, were yet on my father's undisciplined mustache. His denim shirt was open at the throat, and one hand lay on his chest, as if to calm his conflicted heart. Because I'd heard a sign of death was to be seen in the fingernails, in their blueness, I deliberately looked, and for years afterwards I'd check my own fingernails often to see if they were blue and I might be dying and nobody else knew. My mother's hand-quilted spreads were my father's covers against the cold in the room.

My brother brought me to Daddy's bedside to say good-bye. Daddy weak and me trembling, we met for the last time. He knew it was his youngest, and he took my hand and said his last words to me.

"Baby, be a good boy."

Someone sent me onto the front porch, and when my daddy died I was up in the branches of a cedar tree.

As I reflect on my daddy's life over those last six months, I'm reminded of his continuing attentiveness to news about the coming war in Europe, some of which he heard on a neighbor's Motorola or Zenith, for we had no radio of our own. Other news he picked up second-hand on trips into town, gathered from men working around the cotton-gin, or from other farmers sitting on benches in the grocery store, or maybe waiting to cash a check at the bank. But today it still surprises me to consider how faithfully the old man kept up his interest in those distant events in the final months of his life. I know Daddy liked to talk, and I've come to place him among those dirt-poor farmers I've known who, though certainly no better educated than my daddy, were nevertheless deeply interested in ideas we might suppose foreign to them and their daily lives, ideas about a larger world than the one they plowed, planted, and harvested. So I never thought it inconsistent in his character when I reasoned about Daddy's sense of himself as a citizen-farmer with more on his mind than the row he was plowing or the rain he needed on his cotton fields. Once in later years I found among my dad's papers the receipts he'd saved after paying his poll taxes, some going all the way back to Mississippi. In 1891, 1892, and 1894, for three examples, he paid each year a two-dollar poll tax to the Sheriff's Office in Franklin County, Mississippi, obliging them to let him exercise his right as a citizen to vote.

Chapter 5

THE ALLEY OF BAD GUYS

If you'd asked me in the winter of 1940 whether the earth were flat or round, I'd have had a fifty-fifty chance of guessing correctly. At the same time I was sure about one feature of the globe: it had got wrestled upside down from what it used to be. My world was on its head.

Only weeks before I'd started to give it any thought, my world was as familiar as the face I saw in a mirror each morning. The house I lived in, for example, held no secrets from me. It was the house I was born in, and I knew every clapboard and shingle of the house so well I could have put them together again if a tornado struck. I'd played around every corner, and I'd spent stolen hours underneath the house where the ground was dry and the dust occasionally revealed a brass button, an old green key, or some red glass melted into odd shapes in a fire long ago. Our house was solitary, the nearest neighbor's house a mile away along dirt roads. The intervals between houses gave you room to run and play in the sun where cotton and corn grew in the fields. And at night there was darkness untouched by electricity so the sky flooded with stars, while the Milky Way flowed among them. At night people's voices and sounds came from far away, faint as the people you couldn't see. Anytime or anyplace my mother said, "Let's go to the house," I knew she was talking about home.

But now "home" was not the same even for Momma. Her husband, my daddy, now gone, she was unable to handle the work of a tenant farm by herself, a woman, even though her work on a Texas cotton and cattle farm had been taken for granted. As a girl she had cooked and cleaned and washed and sewed and milked cows and picked cotton. Even though Mr. David asked her to stay on at least until summer, she recognized that winter she'd have to make a new life for her and me by "moving to town."

Everything in town was different and strange as a circus. I felt like I was just visiting in the piece of a house where our furniture was stored until we could put it in a wagon and move back to the country. I couldn't sleep at night because the house made funny noises, and people moved about on the other side of our walls after we'd gone to bed. The teen-age girls over there stayed up late at night and played popular music on their radio, none of which I'd ever heard tell of. Because we'd never had electricity in the country, I found the naked light bulbs hanging from our ceilings to be an embarrassment of light; I missed the soft circle of light made by our coal-oil lamps when I read a Superman comic. Everybody else had electricity up and down the street in front of our house, their lights resembling a train passing in the night, and there was even a light on a pole that shined down on the street and in my window after dark. I guessed when you had so many neighbors, you had to keep them from running into each other in the dark. Soon I was to find in town you couldn't even see the Big Dipper in the night sky anymore. The kind of fear I once had in the dark I now felt in the daylight.

A few days after Christmas some boys began to play with a football in the lot next door to our house. Since there were gopher holes and mounds all over the lot, the boys played a game that probably resembled rugby more than football, though I was unfamiliar with either game. They fell down more than not, running being hazardous among the gopher holes, and everyone else piled on a runner when he fell, until the football sprang free and set off a new pursuit and capture. The weather was cold, so my mother forbade me to play on the lot, as I had been somewhat ill during Christmas. All I could do was stand on the porch and watch the boys scuffle, and wonder if the game had rules or they just made it up because somebody got a football for Christmas.

The football game climaxed in a fit of quarreling and yelling after a loud, bone-crunching pileup resulted in one boy going home crying. He trotted past our house, his wailing and crying so self-hypnotizing he didn't notice me on the porch, disappearing along the street before any of his buddies left the gopher-patch. After a few minutes five boys, one tossing up the football, came along the street, scuffling, as if the racket in the game had not satisfied their need for sport. I watched them approach with the feeling of unease I got after a thunderstorm rolled over, but at the same time I couldn't make myself flee inside the house.

Two of the boys kept on walking along the street, but three of them stopped and looked at me up on my porch. The one with the football wore an adult-sized sweater with sleeves dangling beyond his wrists as if they'd been stretched by a tackler during the game. He stepped up onto our yard where the grass was frozen.

"Hey you, boy," he called.

"What?"

"What'cha doing up on that porch?"

"I've got the flu," I said.

"You don't look sick as no dog to me," he said. He turned around and pitched the football to one of the other boys. "I got that football for Christmas."

"It looks like a good one," I said. "I got a drum for Christmas."

"Shoot, you better not bring no drum to school or you won't have it."

He turned around and joined the other boys in the street who were dropping the football and chasing it wherever it tumbled. They recovered the ball and went off along the street without looking back. I'd never thought about taking my drum to school, but his warning reminded me I'd have to take myself there in a day or two. I sure wished I could have Miss Shull for my teacher.

Since truant officers didn't pursue a child whose daddy died, I'd missed over a month of school. But ready or not on the morning following New Years Day, I ate my pre-school breakfast with my mother without any knowledge about behavior expected of me at this Hubbard school; if I had an opinion, it was disguised as anxiety.

I was eating a bun of shredded wheat that looked like a small whale floating belly up in a bowl of milk. Usually at breakfast I read from the Nabisco Shredded Wheat carton, because it had a picture of Niagara Falls on the side of the box, and provided funny cardboard dividers between levels of cereal. Today my anxiety about the new school was compounded by the music coming through our kitchen wall from the other piece of the house. Of late the teenage girls had become fans of a popular song titled "Billy Boy." Radio stations played over and over the song's own repeated lines: "Billy Boy, Billy Boy, Where Have You Been, Charming Billy?" I'd heard the lyrics so often they echoed through my head when I wasn't thinking of something worth my time.

"I wish I'd never started to school in the first place," I said to my mother. "Then I'd be too big for the seats, and the teacher'd tell me to get out, and didn't I have a home?"

"Baby, everybody has to go to school, get an education," said my mother. "That's the law nowadays." She picked up our bowls and started to clear the table. "My mother used to say she hoped it'd be a law one day to make kids go to school. That way, their daddy couldn't make them stay out of school to work in the fields. You'll be glad you went to school when you're bigger, you wait and see."

"No, I won't neither," I said. "I'll work in a hamburger joint like Mr. Truly's in town, and not one person will know who I am and pick at me."

I pushed back my chair from the table and got up, knowing my choices in the matter were as limited as my time to think about them. My mother came and placed her hands on my shoulders and looked me over. She was wearing her red hair shorter these days, maybe barbering it herself, and she'd got herself a pair of eye-glasses, bought off a display rack at the drug store. They made me think of ovals cut from a pane of clear glass, held on her nose without metal frames, just thin metallic temple pieces looping behind her ears. I thought her eyes seemed to swim behind the transparent lenses like marbles in a glass of water, but I never mentioned it. For myself, I was wearing my best overalls with the diamond patch on the breast pocket. My white shirt was clean and freshly ironed by my mother. I had on a new pair of brown laced-over-the-foot oxford shoes that she'd probably bought on credit since we moved to Hubbard. My mother had worried about putting me in a school with kids from high-toned town families. It was important that I look neat. The best she could do was present me neat and decent on my first day at the school, both those words meaning the same thing in her dictionary if she'd had one.

"If you behave as good as you look today, you'll be alright," she lectured me. Little did she know, of course, merely being a mother.

I don't remember it if my teacher at Hubbard Elementary took one look down her nose at me, standing there with my ears jugged out and wearing my new oxfords, and said, "Well, since this new boy appears neat and decent, we'll assign him to the horrid second grade and confine him on the fiendish second floor," but that's where she sent me, probably after gnashing her teeth over my two report cards from Miss Shull, showing a mixture of good works and faithless absenteeism. My new teacher led me up the stairs and assigned me to a seat in the middle of the room where everybody could keep an eye on me, as if I looked like I'd run away before recess.

Without a doubt, the term I spent at Hubbard Elementary from January to June, 1940, was the strangest, most disturbed chapter in my life as a kid, largely because I drifted through it on my own for the first time, like a cork tossed overboard, my usual minders occupied elsewhere. My sister Lucy had gone to take up her married life with Mr. J.D. Bilton, and my sister Maidie had found a job on the Gulf coast. Of course, my mother at the age of thirty-seven now faced the problem of making a living for us in town, a new job each week being her solution. The jobs available to a country woman of few skills and little education required her to clean other people's houses, do their washing and ironing and cooking, and babysit old ladies on pensions. Most days she'd be gone from home all day, leaving in the mornings as I left for school clutching my sack lunch, returning at supper time. I was the original latchkey kid.

My route to school, shorter by half than the wayward paths in the country, was now city streets and sidewalks, which for a few days I walked like a new recruit squaring the parade ground. Then one day I discovered the usefulness and excitement of back alleys. First off, an alley cut corners, skirted the main drag of the streets, gave access to cross-lot pathways, thereby saving travel time. Also, maybe more promising of excellent adventure, there was a mystery about going "behind the lines," as it were, walking behind the backs of people and their houses and their car sheds. At that time, people owned one car, one car shed. There was good stuff, often not quite "respectable," to look at in an alley. Some people tossed perfectly fine throwaways into their garbage cans or slung them behind their fences. You could find broken toys or kitchen supplies or busted furniture. Once I toyed with rescuing from a tin bucket a fine pair of aging cowboy boots, only bent and leaned over by scuffed-down heels as if worn by a bow-legged cowpoke. On another day I came upon a saddled, dozing horse tied to a fence paling. However, as I was soon to find out, I was not the only adventurer of the alleys.

Hubbard Elementary had furnished me asylum for two weeks and I'd not made a friend. I'm sure some of the teachers must have urged me to get out into the schoolyard and mingle in the hurly-burly of recess. But the school and its routines were so alien to me that I shrunk from taking part. As a grammar school building, it must have been a pride to the city, but the very building itself intimidated me; it was huge, two-storied, a fortress of red brick, with slanted red tile roof. A score or more of tall windows made a light-giving procession around both tiers of the building, though to me they appeared to glower down like hooded eyes. My old white-painted wood schoolhouse at Cottonwood could have fitted into the first floor of Hubbard grammar school and not felt crowded for room.

And there were as many children in the first two or three grades as had attended all the grades at my former school. The schoolyard organization, too, was strange to me. Girls played on one side of the school-ground, and boys played on the opposite side. Girls and boys only mingled together at the water fountains, a swampy area near the back doors where several shiny faucets sometimes jetted and sometimes sprayed water above a porcelain trough and among the drinkers.

Trouble came like unwanted company the day I found a set of bed springs in my favorite alley. I had spotted the bed springs on my way to school in the morning, and I was delighted to find them still there on my way home. They leaned against the boards of a weathered fence like a homeless family, a stained and faded mattress, a clutter of bed slats, and the biggest bed springs I'd ever seen in my whole life. Those springs could have accommodated a sleeping giant. And most of the metal coils were still in place. When I pushed down on the coils, they sprang back smartly with a nice zinging sound, almost like some musical instrument. Only a few of the coils were sprung out of shape so they spiraled up like ugly fish hooks. The more I played with the bed springs, the more I considered somehow taking them home with me. My mother often complained about the narrow bed I had to sleep on, me a growing boy without room to turn over at night. These springs would make a grand bed; I'd just have to be wary of the fish hooks.

I hung my book satchel around my neck and across my chest, and began to drag the bed springs a little at a time, lift one end and drag, lift the end and drag. I had made a short trail in the dirt when I saw several boys coming along the alley toward me. They appeared interested.

"Hey, kid. What'cha got there?" It was the boy who got the football for Christmas. He still wore the sweater with sleeves too long for him, as if his mother hadn't noticed.

"A bed springs," I said.

The boys came up and looked at the springs and poked at the coils. One boy shook the springs vigorously, and several coils twisted out like fish hooks.

"Where you taking these good old bed springs?"

"Home," I said.

All the boys were quiet and appeared to study the situation.

"Hey, kid. What's your name?" The boy who owned the football gave me a little push, and I backed up against the bed springs.

"My name's Leon," I said.

"His name's Leon," he said to the other boys and, to my astonishment, they fell to laughing and stomping their feet around, as if they were dancing a jig.

"Take it away, Leon!" One boy was shouting and pointing at me.

The other boys took up the cry: "Take it away, Le-e-e-o-o-o-n!"

I looked on this frolicking performance in amazement. Because we hadn't owned a radio and listened to popular country music right out of Waco and Fort Worth, I'd never heard the celebrated Texas bandleader, Bob Wills, and his Western swing band, the Texas Playboys. One of the many things I didn't know about Bob Wills and the Texas Playboys was in that very year of 1940 they were recording their most famous song, "San Antonio Rose." Most important to me at the moment, however, was my ignorance of a well-known habit of Mr. Wills. I didn't know that one of the Playboys was a steel guitar player named Leon McAuliffe, and how could I know that when Mr. Leon McAuliffe furiously launched into a lively, toe-tapping solo, Mr. Bob Wills would yell out a rowdy, "Take it away, Le-e-o-o-n!"

The trio of boys quieted down except for random sniggering. Apparently a new idea had appeared like a light bulb over the head of their leader.

"You stealing these good old bed springs, Leon?"

"I'm taking them home," I said.

"I'll dang bet you didn't ask Mr. Jones if you could have them," he said. "That makes you a robber."

"Somebody throwed them out here in the alley," I said.

The boy pushed up against me and made me stumble against the springs. My book satchel pulled awkwardly against my neck. My writing tablet dropped out and fell to the ground.

"I think you're a robber, and we're gonna tell Old Man Mackelroy. He's constable, and he's gonna come take you to jail. You ever been in jail, Leon?" He turned to his companions. "Take it away, Leon! Ain't that right?"

One of the boys had picked up my writing tablet, glanced at it, and handed it to the boy who owned the football.

"Billy Joe, he's in second grade."

"Who's your teacher, Leon?" Billy Joe asked.

I told him. He was looking in my tablet.

"How come you're writing cursive and you're in second grade?"

"I learned it because of my sister," I said.

He showed the tablet to the other boys.

"Leon's already writing cursive in the second grade, and he's a robber," he said.

"It's my tablet," I said.

He stuffed the tablet into my book satchel, and pulled down hard on the strap and yanked my neck with enough force to leave a red mark on the back of my neck.

"That's pretty good cursive for a robber," he said. "We got to go play ball, but if we see you robbing that old bed springs along down the road, we're gonna tell Old Man Mackelroy."

From down the alley, the boys turned and shouted, "Take it away, Le-e-e-o-o-n!" I could hear their laughter as they were disappearing around the next corner.

I told my mother about the bed springs, but she only said, "Don't mess with old junk in that alley, or you'll get blood poison, and where would we be then?"

The next week found me back at my usual stand at school: up against the wall. While the other kids rushed outside to the playgrounds, shoving each other from the back, gushing shouts and laughter, I tried to merge with the newel posts of the staircase. I had developed no second-grade social graces, and fear of playground toughs immobilized me.

I did become skilled at "being sick." Most of the time my mother worked all day, meaning she wouldn't return home for lunch, but on rare occasions when she had no job, she allowed me to come home for lunch. I'd run all the way, leaping over frozen puddles on the sidewalk, eat lunch, and run back to school in time for my teacher to call the roll. Thus, one day at home for lunch I began to think I was sick. After a few minutes, I located the source of sickness.

"My stomach hurts, "I announced.

"You probably eat too fast," Momma said. "I don't think it's a good idea, you running home and gobbling down your food like some old hog. Why can't you sit with the other kids, eat your peanut butter sandwiches? Wouldn't that be better?"

"I guess," I said. "But my stomach hurts. Maybe I have appendicitis?"

By this time Momma was up from the table, placing the butter dish in our ice box. She didn't become panicky or vexed by my self-diagnosis.

"Where does it hurt? Point your finger to the place it hurts."

I put my finger more or less on my belly button.

"Maybe I'll need an operation?"

"That's not where your appendicitis is. It's on your left side," she pointed out.

"I guess I'd better lay down, just in case."

Momma helped me to my bed and gave me a wet cloth to put on my forehead. My only fear was she'd want to give me castor oil or Fletcher's Castoria for my stomach. But she didn't, maybe because she knew more than she let on about my illness.

I took a note to my teacher the next morning, explaining my absence. She didn't fuss, only gave me a list of sums I'd missed and told me to total them up for her. Since I was good with numbers, I quickly caught up with my classmates. Why, I thought, couldn't I do like this all the time, just come to school in the mornings, catch up on the teacher's work next day? Such thinking emboldened me, and a few days later I walked up to my teacher's desk, my book satchel in my hand, while the class was scissoring and pasting magazine pictures on construction paper.

"I have a awful stomach ache," I heard myself say. "I may have appendicitis." I pointed to my left side and grimaced. "Can I be excused?"

Approximately twenty-five sets of hands became still and the same number of heads raised up, eyes staring at this unusual situation. Perhaps many of them wondered why they'd never had appendicitis, others just figured they'd been right about me deserting before recess.

When I arrived home with another case of appendicitis, my mother was not pleased. Of course, the first thing she did was set me down and feel my forehead for fever. No fever. Then she pushed gently on my left side, feeling for pain. No pain. She didn't become angry, just serious and worried-looking. She pulled up a chair next to mine, reached her new glasses out of her apron pocket and set them on her nose. I had to watch the marbles floating in water behind her lenses.

"Baby, I know you don't like your school," she began. "You'd like to be back with your friends at Cottonwood. I know you miss Kenneth and Dixie Lynn and them. But your mama couldn't help it we had to move. When Daddy passed away, we'd only got ourselves to look out for us." She took her glasses off and got a handkerchief and wiped them and her eyes. I was sure afraid she was going to carry on, but she didn't. "Don't you think your momma'd like to be back at Mr. David's? But I've got to work these places here in town, got to try and scrape together enough for us to live on." She placed her palm on my forehead just in case the fever had set in. "So you can't stay out of school. I can't see how in the world your teacher can pass you, if you don't get your spelling and arithmetic." I guess she thought she'd preached enough, because she slipped her glasses off and folded them up and put them into her apron pocket. She patted me on the cheek and smiled now the sermon had ended. "It's like your grandpa always says, 'You sure can't fish, if you don't dig some bait.'"

Next morning I was back at school. When I handed my mother's note to my teacher, I said, "Momma says I'm well now."

Texas weather in February and March can be chilly out in the wind and

misting rain. "Cold enough to freeze the horns off a Billy goat." The sometimes freezing weather gave me an excuse for staying inside the school house during recess; the equally frigid Northers also made my daily hikes to and from school into hardship. I'd zipper my coat up to my chin, stuff my hands into the pockets, and wrench the flaps on my cap down around my stone-cold ears.

The ground remained frozen, and where the rain left puddles on the sidewalk, even on the dirt streets in the alleys, thick, glittering sheets of ice formed on top of the water. There'd be veins of air within the ice, creating otherworldly crystal images, and frost sprinkled its cold dust around the edges of the icy puddles. I loved chunking rocks at the ice. As it turned out, most of the things I liked to do on the way to school, other boys did also.

One morning I was not paying attention, sauntering my reluctant way to school, the tune "Billy Boy, Where Have You Been, Charming Billy" murmuring in my head, and I walked up on Billy Joe and his gang breaking ice on the sidewalk. It was like refugees from a carnival having a party. More dangerous, though. They were about a block from the schoolyard, so close there was no worry about making it to school in time for the tardy bell. One boy was breaking ice on a large puddle by stomping it with his boot. Shards of ice had splintered all around. Water splashed each time the boy stomped his foot. Another boy was sailing shards of ice into the street where they shattered like fragments of window panes. Spatters of ice made the street appear full of diamonds in the early morning sunlight. Billy Joe was rolling up the sleeves of his sweater; the sleeves looked wet and his hands were pink with cold.

"Hey, it's Leon," called out the boy throwing ice. "Take it away, Le-e-o-o-n!" he shouted in my direction. He sailed a few panes of ice at me.

"Come over here, kid," said Billy Joe, wiping his hands on the front of his sweater.

LONNIE L.WILLIS

I stopped several feet back of the ice show. My ears and face were cold already.

"What is it?" I asked.

"Leon, you're so dang deef you can't be in no second grade."

"I ain't deef," I said.

"You heard me then," Billy Joe said. "Come on over here. Bring your dang book satchel with you." The other boys just looked, thinking what he was up to.

"What you want?"

He stooped and began to pick up pieces of ice from the puddle. Once he had a stack of them, they were so cold he had to shuffle the stack from hand to hand.

"Bet you never seen no hot ice before," he said. "This here is hot ice, so hot it's smoking. We're digging up this hot ice, going to take this old hot ice to school, show it to the principal. You want to help? Come on." He held out a piece of ice, but it looked freezing cold to me. I knew about cold from the farm where in the winter the trees froze over with ice and chunks fell off after the sun came out.

"Ice is cold," I said. "It ain't hot, just doing nothing but melting in your hand."

He began to move toward me, which I took for a bad sign.

"If this ice ain't hot, then I guess it'll melt down your collar."

Billy Joe rushed me so fast I couldn't get around him. One of the other boys ran up behind and grabbed me around the shoulders, pinning my arms. One of his arms brushed my head and my cap fell off, but I couldn't catch it so it dropped on the ground near our feet. Because my cap was gone, the other boy started breaking ice shards over my head. Some pieces slid down my neck and inside my coat.

74

I tried twisting away from his grasp, but Billy Joe grabbed my collar and yanked it and shoved his stack of ice down my back. The shock of ice down my back on this cold morning was a jolt like to freeze my blood. But the jolt of ice was so rousing I burst free of them with a desperate strength I'd not had otherwise.

I ran down the sidewalk like a cat out of a bag, furiously propelled by anger and fright. My book satchel banged against my rear end, but I flew. My feet pounded the sidewalk. My arms pistoned from side to side. Ice melting down my back fueled my reckless, swift motion headlong. But even as I ran, I heard feet pounding behind me. Billy Joe was in pursuit.

"Leon, I'm gonna make you eat your dang cap," he was shouting, his breathless voice rising, falling, gasping with his angry running. He was getting so close I could imagine him about to grab me from behind.

We came to the end of the sidewalk. Where the cement ended, the hard dirt fell away, so the street was about two feet lower than the cement sidewalk.

I stopped suddenly just as the cement ended, and fell to my knees. Right behind me, Billy Joe had no time to stop. He tripped over my kneeling body and flew through the air like a diver off a board, head first toward the street below. By the time he landed, I was seated in my classroom listening to roll call.

When my teacher called my name, I spoke up briskly: "Here!"

In the days following, Billy Joe seemed to avoid me, and I eased onto the playground for occasional games. I began to run around and get chased by boys. I mingled at the sump of a water fountain. Got my shirt wet. Made faces at girls.

But one day a few weeks afterwards I arrived home to find my mother already there. I had expected her to be at work, doing somebody's laundry, but she was in the front room seated at her Singer sewing machine, pedaling it and sewing buttons onto a shirt. She was grinning at me like she had a big surprise. I knew it wasn't my eight-year-old birthday surprise, for that was over a month away.

"Guess what," she said. "We're going on a little trip. You remember your Aunt Anna? She was your daddy's sister, and she's been under the weather lately. Some of her kids, they want somebody to come and stay with her for about a month. They asked me if I'd do it, and I said yes, you and me would. You can bring your funny books, and you won't be going to school, just stay out about three weeks."

I let my book satchel dangle on the floor at my feet.

"Ain't that a jim-dandy surprise?" she said.

"Dang!" I thought.

Chapter 6

"HOLY MACKEREL! HERE THEY COME!"

Some uncle or other's Ford Model A carried us along a dirt road, winter-blanched corn stalks bent into curious shapes in the fields on either side of us, shapes which made me think of old men bending over to pick corn from the frozen ground. My mother and I were going to stay for a while with Aunt Anna who lived by herself in a house outside of town, not far, but really in the country. There was still plenty winter in the air, clouds hovering, to make me wish for snow, not that we ever got much of it. Wearing one of her best print dresses, and her one nice coat, my mother sat in the front seat beside the driver, and their heads rose above the seat-backs and carried on gossip about grown-ups that murmured outside my range of interest. An ancient cardboard Woolworth's suitcase rested on the back seat beside me, and trembled with the movement of the car. A length of fuzzy binder twine looped around the suitcase to keep its lid from popping open. My own head was "stuck in a funny book," as my mother often phrased it, partly because she didn't understand my obsession, partly in disapproval. She suspected the crudely drawn and vividly colored pulpy books were bad for me and not only by ruining my eyes.

Comic books, or "funny books" as grownups called them, had become a refuge for me. I owned no "real" books like *Tom Sawyer* or *Treasure Island* to read. Of course, my father's Bible with the steel engravings had gone out into the family somewhere, so was no longer available to me. I couldn't go to the movies by myself at the age of seven, the television in a box hadn't been invented, and the radio played war news from over the waters ready to disturb my dreams at night. Thus, I'd found a means of escape by investing my imagination in comic books with their brilliant covers, their gritty but hypnotizing drawings, and characters that slipped the bounds of real life by flying, changing shape, becoming invisible, wearing capes and masks, and chanting enigmatic formulas. Because I could neither fly over buildings nor shrink to the size of a doll nor disappear into an invisible boy, I'd learned to escape the constraints of my everyday conditions by hiding among the panels of ten-cent comic books.

"Why don't you throw down that old funny book, Leon?" My mother could see me in the rearview mirror above the windshield. "You'll ruin what's left of your eyes, reading in this car, moving."

Today as we rode through the tail end of winter to Aunt Anna's house, I "had my head stuck in" *Broncho Bill*, "64 full color pages," a just-published 1940 comic book decorated with a cover illustration of a young cowboy--not much older than myself--wearing a white hat, leather chaps, and boots with spurs, while sticking tight as can be in a saddle cinched onto a walleyed midnight-black broncho, sun-fishing up a cloud of dust in a cedar-pole corral. I was fascinated by his leather gloves. They had a red star stitched onto each wrist protector. I needed a pair like them. Unlike me, Broncho Bill didn't need anything but his horse and the pair of six-shooters he wore on the leather belt holding up his bluejeans.

Certainly I understood we were going to stay with my Aunt Anna who was not well, for my mother had explained all that, but I wasn't clear about how long we'd be in her house. And, what's more, I wondered: were there going to be any human beings around? Well, of course, my mother. And Aunt Anna herself. But they didn't play with a football or carry pocket knives or go in the back alley looking for unexpected treasures thrown out of rich people's houses. I only knew I'd not get back to Hubbard Elementary until school was near out, and I was beginning to think I might end up a hermit or something. But it wasn't up to me to decide if I'd pass the second grade or not. So the only thing I had to study to find out what life was all about was my traveling pulp library: Batman, Superman, Popeye, and Little Orphan Annie.

However, at this time in my life I was fascinated by cowboys, having been taken by my sisters back before my daddy died to sit in the dark and watch shoot-outs among boulders and canyons like I'd never seen and run-away stage coaches falling over cliffs in movies featuring Gene Autry and Roy Rogers. So here I was, coming to terms as best I could at the age of seven with these contradicting emotions resulting from a situation in which I'd got what I asked for—leaving school—but now having second thoughts about a life without action. I'd have to miss out on school not only at Cottonwood, but also at Hubbard Elementary, and I found my interest in truancy waning and my memories of outwitting Billy Joe waxing. My only immediate avenue of escape rested with Broncho Bill and his horse Blackie, whose stirring adventures captivated me.

Aunt Anna barely had room for Momma and me. Her house was three rooms, not counting a screened-in porch and a brick chimney, backed up against the littlest garden I'd ever seen, mostly some frost-bitten remains of tomato plants. Plus there were a few white chickens clucking about her yard, looking for rare places in the sun to spread their wings and dust their selves. But as the person who commenced my mother's--and my own--tour of "staying with" needy people, Aunt Anna was perfect. She looked like grandmothers I'd known in magazines, not having any real ones myself, outfitting herself every day in a long apron and ankle-length dresses that barely revealed black leather shoes with tiny holes in the toes forming what I took for flowers. Old women's shoes, I guessed. When Aunt Anna boiled us some oatmeal for breakfast, she made me think of ads for kitchen stoves I'd seen in *Life* magazines.

I couldn't see that Aunt Anna was sick. She was the cheeriest woman I'd ever seen. She and my mother talked over arrangements for helping her get some rest, but I never knew her not to work all day around the house anyway. Her white hair coiled at the back of her head like a knot of silk rope. Probably her eyesight was poor, because her eye-glasses were thicker than my mother's. And yet she saw clearly my own peculiar situation: a seven-year-old boy stranded with two adults wearing kitchen aprons. With a rare sensitivity for an old person she recognized my need to play and run about.

After a breakfast of oatmeal, biscuits, peach preserves, and coffee on our second day with Aunt Anna, she said to my mother, "Bill, why don't you let Leon go down and play in the ditch?"

I didn't know anything about "the ditch," but I could recognize a get-away from the house when I heard it, and was eager to explore.

"Let me go, Momma, and I'll get right back when you call me. If I don't, I won't ever ask again."

Where runoff from rains in the past flowed downhill beyond my aunt's little garden, a gully--cut and deepened by that muddy downhill water--now wandered through a field until it reached a creek some distance from the house. You couldn't see where the ravine emptied into the creek, but the near end, the source of the ditch, was so close to the house and so shallow that Aunt Anna threw her garbage there. Just below the garbage dump's scatter of cans and bottles, the gully widened and deepened into a miniature canyon with twists and bends like the ones you'd see in a Saturday serial about explorers and caves where you could get buried alive.

My mother stood on Aunt Anna's porch and watched me skip off down toward the ditch. Shading her eyes with one hand against the morning sun, she could see the rubbish dump from the house, it was that close. The sight of rusting Del Monte creamstyle-corn cans and discarded Coca Cola bottles apparently made her nervous about my welfare.

"Don't you mess with them old cans," she called after me. "Where all would we be if you got blood poison?"

I spent the first thirty minutes in the ditch fishing around in Aunt Anna's rubbish pile. You never could tell what you might find among castaway belongings. I'd learned that lesson in the allies on my way to Hubbard Elementary. After I kicked the cans around and got them out of the way and wouldn't get blood poison, I found an empty Mrs. Tucker's lard bucket Aunt Anna had washed, but for

81

some unimaginable reason had thrown out, so I began to use it as a receptacle for small treasures. The bucket had a wire handle which made it convenient to carry while I dug with a stick amid the cola bottles and little metal things I uncovered.

Probably every rubbish pile in the world has an old clock in it, and I located one first thing, a nice Waterbury alarm clock with two silver cup-shaped bells on top that waked you up when a metal hammer rattled against them. The hammer was missing, but I found the bells created pleasing musical sounds when tapped with the lip of a Dr Pepper bottle. The metal windup key in the back turned around and around but did not wind anything up, which was no problem, because I learned I could set whatever time I wanted by manually turning the hands on the clock face. I laid the clock in my lard bucket.

With hardly any work at all with my stick I found a pair of wire pliers, rusted closed, and a garden hoe without its handle, and an S-shaped crank for a Model T. Inside a kid's toy bank made to look like a cash register was something that rattled like a dime but turned out to be a penny. Of course, much of the litter was broken glass, as if Aunt Anna couldn't help dropping her dishes or she threw them at somebody. But among the trash were a lot of unbroken soda pop bottles, some really good RC Cola, Coca Cola, and Dr. Pepper bottles, and I collected them into a pile because I could use them to chuck rocks at later on. I put my treasures into the lard can, and carried it and the Model-T crank with me as I began the exploration of the ditch.

The bottom of the gully was wet sand. As I adventured into the ravine, my high-top tennis shoes rolled off a track of dented prints in the sand, which I liked, for I knew in case of great danger I could escape back out by following my footprints. I'd not get lost for sure, even if a big flood came or anything. Soon I found the sides of the ravine were higher than my head and wider than I could touch on either side if I walked in mid-space. The walls of the ditch went straight up, but in places the eroding silt spilled down the walls and formed hillocks of gravel and clods not unlike pretend mountains. I figured earthquakes had made them, which meant I might see one anytime. And in places funny misshapen roots squirmed out of the sides of the ditch, their coils and threads making me think of snakes, so I battled them for a bit with my Model-T crank.

From where I stood I could no longer see the house, so I figured I'd better not go much further into the gully in case my mother called me. Besides, I decided, this was the perfect spot to examine my treasures. The sand was damp, but not muddy, the rough sides of the ditch enclosed me, and I experienced a pleasant knowledge of isolation. There were no sounds to speak of, save for a blue jay's shriek down on the creek. It felt like a secret place. Maybe being a hermit might not be so bad.

I emptied my treasures onto the ground, placed Mrs. Tucker's lard bucket upside down on the moist sand, and sat on it. I took each object in hand and examined it carefully, looking for its use here in my secret hideaway. There seemed to be no use for the rusted pliers. Them I set aside. But the T-Model crank resembled a gun I'd seen at the movies, so I kept it beside the bucket. The clock was the best treasure, if I didn't mind there was no ticking. With a real clock, though, I sure needed a shelf to keep it on the way my mother kept her clock on the dresser where she could tell what time to get ready or when to take the biscuits out. Without any boards to make a shelf, I had to use anything at hand. I punched the T-Model crank into the side of the gully and dislodged a few clods of dirt, then where the clods had been I sculpted a cavity with the garden hoe, and set my clock inside. It stared directly at me from inside its burrow like a hiding animal.

By this time I'd disposed of all my treasures except the toy bank. Thinking it deserved a site equal to my clock, I picked out more clods, let them fall onto the ground, and smoothed the hole in the wall with the hoe. I rattled the coin against the sides of the tin bank and could see it lie across the slot where coins dropped inside, yet I couldn't shake it out. The bank would be just fine inside the little pocket I'd made for it in the wall, but I wanted the penny to carry in the pocket of my jacket. I looked underneath the play cash register and saw it had a round disc which screwed loose to let the bank's owner remove coins if he wanted to buy a comic book at the drugstore. I scraped a bit of rust away with my fingernail, then twisted the disc, and jiggled the penny out and into my hand. This is one fine penny, I thought. It wasn't shiny and bright, and it even had a touch of green here and there, but I didn't care.

This penny was the first money I'd ever found. Not that I got much money anyway, but when I did it came directly from somebody's hand into mine. Maybe I'd always keep this special penny and not spend it even if I had to starve one penny short of a hamburger. Or it might bring me good luck, which I needed. While I was just putting the penny into my coat pocket, I recalled something I'd heard Mr. Waller say back when we lived on the farm with my daddy and them.

"If I had two pennies, I'd rub them together and be rich," he'd said.

Now here I had one penny. I'd need one more. I resolved to watch like a hawk for another penny, and I'd get into my secret place and rub them together and wait for gold and stuff. I'd have to wait and see, because I'd never seen it happen before.

A distraction in the form of my mother's voice brought me back from thoughts of gold.

"Leon, where in the world are you?"

I looked up from where I sat on the lard bucket, and I could see dark, gray clouds moving across the strip of sky above the ravine. Drops of cold rain had drizzled onto my shoulders and head, though I was too carried away with my work in the ditch to notice.

Momma's head appeared above me.

"Don't you know to come in out of the rain? You want to be like an old turkey, stand in the rain with your mouth gaped open and drown?"

"No, ma'am," I called. "I'm coming." The marvels of the ditch had to wait.

A slow, cold Texas rain kept me inside the house for the next two days.

Aunt Anna opened cans of Carnation condensed milk, poured the milk into soup bowls, and showed me how to dip graham crackers into the milk. This tasty sweet was new to me, and I gorged myself on it so much that it almost took my mind off the ditch. She didn't seem to mind that I sat all morning at her kitchen table dunking graham crackers and reading *Broncho Bill*. It was a way of keeping me occupied while she and Momma ironed and cleaned and gossiped about family matters.

Cooped up as she was with my daddy's own sister, Momma tended to carry on more than usual. While the rain sounded on the roof, the water spouting from the gutters, she'd get to talking about how Daddy passed away, where he was buried and all, telling the story I'd had to listen to so many times it made my insides hurt.

"Anna, it just about killed me when I seen that old hearse coming up the dirt road from the Lees' house, knowing it would turn in our yard." Momma and Aunt Anna were cutting "quilt pieces" out of old dresses and ladies' skirts, useless except for my aunt to piece into quilts, which she used to cover her bed and sold occasional ones to people who thought her quilts were pretty. Aunt Anna nodded her head as if she could see that old hearse herself.

"You'all was close, you and Luther," she said.

"We was standing in the yard, me and Leon, beside some froze flower beds there. Both of us watched the men from the funeral home drive up and come around that big mesquite tree and back up the hearse at the front porch. All I could do, I just hugged the baby, and we was both crying. Marvin and the men come out of the house to talk to the undertakers."

That day I'd stood in the yard with Momma and watched the hearse come to take my daddy seemed a long time away to me. If I let myself, especially on occasions when Momma carried on and I had no choice but to listen while she recited the details of his passing, I could see somewhere in my mind the long, dark automobile with black curtains in the windows, its rear door, heavy and egg-shaped, opening up, and the steel rollers and the purple fabric carpet within.

But I didn't think very often about those things. Mostly, when I thought about Daddy it was the family I missed, all of us living back on Mr. David's place, and all of us happy. I was in a different world now, with new people, and, especially, new problems.

My biggest problem, I'd decided, was how to keep from becoming a hermit. I even looked in a mirror once to be sure my hair wasn't getting long.

Aunt Anna was using up her supply of graham crackers and condensed milk on me, but the rain kept her and Momma and me closed in on all sides. By the third day in the house I'd read *Broncho Bill* three times, front to back. Little Orphan Annie wore thin after two readings, I found, and her eyes bothered me, so I colored some of them with a pencil. I was missing the ditch bad.

The next day was clear, and sunshine spread across our breakfast table. I was eager to get to the ditch and see if my secret place was under water, but my mother said it would be muddy down there and I'd be a sight when I come back. Nothing to do but eat my oatmeal and biscuits, listening all the while to Aunt Anna and Momma discuss the war news they'd heard on the radio. Aunt Anna was worried about some of her boys going off to the Army or Navy and be killed.

"I don't see why we can't let the folks over the water settle their own wars without us mixing up in it," she said.

"That's right," agreed my mother, "but they're bound and determined to get us in a fix."

I was afraid they'd talk me into bad dreams if they got to talking about war, unless I could use something as an excuse to get me out of the house.

"Momma, do you think the Germans will send bombers over here and blow us up?"

"I don't guess so, Baby," she said, but I could tell she worried about my bad dreams.

"Maybe I better go play," I suggested.

My mother was right about the ditch having become a muddy sight. Two or more days of rain had created the kind of streams that made the gully what it was in the first place. Puddles of water remained along the ground, reflecting the sky and early-morning sun in wet mirrors. In my secret place Mrs. Tucker's lard bucket poked up from a pool of water like a lighthouse. My toy bank was safe in its notch on the other side of the gully, but the clock had fallen off its perch and lay on a muddy slope at the far side of the pool. How was I to retrieve my clock from that mess? There was no way I'd get out of the house again if I stomped through the puddles, then waded the pool of water. My mother always carried on when she noticed things like muddy tennis shoes and soppy overalls, even if they didn't bother me the least bit.

Looking down into the gully at the site where my clock lay, upside down on the shore of a pool of rainwater, I suddenly remembered an episode from the adventures of Broncho Bill. I ran back to the house and, without raising enough suspicion to restrain me in the sewing circle, I collected *Broncho Bill* from the kitchen and hurried back to the ditch. Sitting at the brink of the gully, I thumbed a few pages of the comic and found the episode I'd recalled. I read: "Dad and Nell still are searching the Powder River mountains for Bill who, fleeing from Rawlins' men on one of their own horses, now draws to a sudden stop at the brink of a deep wide chasm."

The four-color pictures that accompanied this written text excited my imagination but also suggested to me a practical solution to my problem: how to retrieve my clock. A double-wide panel showed Bill standing on the edge of a precipice, throwing his lariat across the gorge, and looping a tall rock on the opposite side: "Quickly he uncoils a lariat from the bandit's saddle and ropes a pinnacle rock on the other side." Because the outlaws were spurring their horses down on Bill, firing their Winchesters in the air, the next panel showed him hurriedly tying one end of the lariat to a nearby pine tree: "Holy mackerel! Here they come!" The next panel pictured Bill, his rifle scabbard slung over his back, now hanging along the rope mid-way across the chasm. "If I can only reach the other side before they get here," he exclaimed.

Where could I get a rope?

I rolled up my comic book and put it into a pocket of my jacket and surveyed my nearby surroundings. If my penny was really lucky, like I thought, I'd spot a rope. Off to my right in the ditch was Aunt Anna's trash, directly behind me was her woodpile, her axe stuck into a log, and to my left lay an overturned iron wash pot like the one my mother used to boil her clothes when we lived at Mr. David's. I guessed Aunt Anna, who was supposed to be sickly, must cut her own stove wood and wash her own clothes. I thought I could imagine her doing that alright. Beyond her iron wash pot two metal posts sticking in the ground were joined by two strands of rope. Her clothes line.

The rope turned out to be clothes-line rope, strong enough to hold wet sheets and dresses off the ground while drying in the sun, but not made for hobbling a horse. I discovered, however, that Aunt

Anna's rope was twice as long as I needed and in excellent shape judging by how it played out straight when I yanked on it several times. So I untied it from the posts, coiled it up into a loop, and went looking for a pinnacle or a pine tree on the other side of the ditch. This would prove to be the first of several adventures in my life involving ropes and high places.

Lucky for my current purpose a bobwire fence meandered along parallel to the far side of the gully, separating it from a field as it carved its way toward the creek. At a point where the gully was about six feet wide I saw a fence post on the far side, a useful substitute for a pinnacle rock. As I had no experience in twirling a lariat, I took my coil of rope, galloped around the trash pile, and went to the fence post, well fixed in the ground. Just as Broncho Bill did at the pine tree, I fastened one end of my rope to the fence post, tying a knot I'd learned from my sister. Then I flung the wadded up rope across the gully, uncoiling as it went, and landed most of it on the other side.

Back again on the other side of the gully, I quickly realized I had nothing to anchor the rope. No tree. No horse. No rock. I had one end attached on the distant side, but here I stood like a dope, holding the loose end of a rope I hoped to traverse a chasm on. How was I going to act out Bill's hand-over-hand crossing of the chasm on a rope attached on only one side? Briefly I considered giving up and calling my mother and asking for help getting my clock. I stuffed one hand into my pocket to get it warm and brushed against *Broncho Bill*. That touch activated in my mind a picture of Bill hanging on a rope in the very face of death by flying bullets. He didn't call his mother, and neither would I. Actually this chasm's width was no more than the length of Bill's horse, about that deep, and I had rope to spare.

I must have something to tie up to, that was certain. I noticed Aunt Anna's clothes-line posts, but my rope wouldn't reach that far. I went and examined the logs in her woodpile, but they were short and light, sawed into firewood. Then I saw her iron washpot, heavy as a tub full of water. It was black with soot, turned upside down in the ashes from Aunt Anna's last washing. The kettle resembled a castiron turtle, heavy as a truck.

I tipped the pot onto its belly with a stick and began to shove it over the ground, luckily still oozy from the rains. Three stubby legs on the bottom dug a trail as I pushed and pulled, the hardest job I'd ever had, though not as hard as my resolve. Two handles had been welded near the top of the pot, making it possible for two persons to lug it onto a fire. When I had it near the rim of the ditch, I was out of breath and while I rested I saw that my hands were black with soot. I could wash them later, so I wasn't worried.

Curiously, the only thing that worried me was the chance that my mother would show up before I rescued my clock.

The heavy washpot sat boulder-like on the edge of the chasm waiting to anchor my rope. I gave the rope a few jerks to be sure the fence post on the other side was secure, then threaded my end of the rope through one of the handles on the pot. I knotted the rope. It was tight on the handle. I looked with pleasure along my rope stretched the width of the ditch. It was neither as wide nor as deep as Broncho Bill's chasm, but I only needed to get most of the way across, drop beyond the pool of water, and collect my clock, maybe also get the toy bank.

Looking down from the rim, however, for a minute or two I felt giddy, maybe from the height, maybe from nerves. Out in front of me stretched the rope, and the scene with Broncho Bill dangling in mid-chasm flashed into my mind. Back behind me, back at the house, my mother waited, maybe getting anxious. Time to get my clock. I stooped down at the rim of the ditch, leaned outward a bit, and grasped the rope with two hands.

"Holy mackerel!" I shouted, "Here they come!"

And I leapt into the ditch.

There was a momentary feeling of elation as I hung on the rope--I've done it!--and then the washtub jerked over the edge of the chasm and pulled it and me into the pool of water below. It was not far to fall, not even enough to knock the breath out of me, but I landed backwards into the water and heard the kettle thump into the mud nearby. I was stunned more by the cold water, with the few seconds I lay soaking, than by the fall itself. Somewhere in the distance I heard a blue jay shriek.

Getting up on my feet, standing in the puddle, holding my arms out from my body, I did the typical after-catastrophe inspection. My head didn't hurt, though my hair was wet, leaking puddle water down my collar. No broken bones in my arms. My hands were soot black, but wiping them on the seat of my overalls left them heavy with mud. I moved my legs and feet. I was a creature of mud from the waist down. My tennis shoes were submerged in muddy water, and my soaked pants legs began to shiver in the cold.

"Dang!" I said out loud.

I don't recall that I cried. I did stand on Aunt Anna's porch and wail, because I suspected I'd gotten into a situation too big for me to handle by myself. Mamma and Aunt Anna rushed out of the door immediately and stared at me. I must have looked like a mud statue.

"Lord a' mercy, Leon, what happened to you?" My mother wanted to touch me, but she seemed afraid to, maybe thinking there were broken bones in me somewhere. She knelt in front of me and took a needle she'd been sewing with out of her mouth and pinned it in her apron. "What in the world have you done to yourself?"

"My rope I'd tied to Aunt Anna's washpot pulled me in the ditch where my clock was, and the puddle soaked me," I explained quickly. "But I'm alright." I hoped my story would get me some dry clothes, because I was wet, froze up, and about to pee. Water pooled at my feet.

"Let's get this mess off you, then we'll see if you need your britches switched," said my mother. "I hope you ain't made a mess of Aunt Anna's washpot."

A noise made me notice Aunt Anna standing behind Momma. At first I took it she was about to cry. Then, I knew she was laughing. I couldn't believe it. She was a grandmother and still laughing so hard tears came out her eyes. I guessed she was laughing at the way I looked, standing there making a mud puddle, water soaked like a drowned rat.

I only got to make one more trip to the ditch, just before we left Aunt Anna's house and went to stay with an old woman on a pension. The weather had warmed up, winter giving way to spring, and I'd been in the house a lot. In the meantime I'd overheard Momma and Aunt Anna talk about the trouble they'd had getting the washpot out of the ditch and back up to the wood pile. My conscience talking, I guess.

Chapter 7

CLAIM JUMPERS ON THE RAILROAD TRACK

Momma and me had been staying with this meanest old woman alive for over a week to make some money, when one morning Mr. Waller and my uncle, Wylie Godwin, drove up to her front door in Wylie's Model-A Ford. They both wore overalls and work shoes, so the meanest old woman wouldn't allow Momma's visitors to come inside her house for fear they'd walk on her rugs. We all stood out on the porch and talked. Mr. Waller wanted to know why in the world Momma and me didn't come and live with all of them at a place called Union High. Uncle Wylie said they had a big house on Mr. Joe Keitt's place, and he was a banker, so come on ahead. Of course, I was prepared to go anywhere at the moment's notice, even Europe, because my life couldn't be any more miserable if I was being bombed from the sky every day.

"Guess you'all didn't know Artie called around to find somebody'd come and stay with her sister," said Momma. "She's got a baby coming, and needs somebody to set up with her."

Then Momma told them we'd supposed to go stay a couple of weeks over in the town of Corsicana. Momma could help this lady with washing diapers and rocking the dopey kid. I heard Momma tell Mr. Waller that after this job we'd move our stuff down to Union High, and that would be so-long to the meanest old woman on earth. She was so mean she wouldn't let me play outside in her yard, said I'd push little cars around and make all her dirt wash away. The old lady spent most of her time in a dark parlor, gabbling at me for the sin of being a kid, while my mother cleaned up specks of dust from the chair cushions.

Bad luck was going around in my life then like the measles, which I blamed on losing my lucky penny in the ditch behind Aunt Anna's wood pile. Example: there was only one week when I was permitted to take my book satchel and walk across town back to Hubbard Elementary, not that I had time to enjoy anything when I got there, except people looking at me like I was a hermit. But I did get a couple of whopping surprises.

The biggest one arrived with a bang on the school ground when I literally ran into Billy Joe during a fast game of "Crack the Whip," where you get slung on the ground. We both were laying on the ground figuring out if we were dead or alive after knocking our heads together, and Billy Joe looked over at me and said, "Dang it all, Leon, you and me is cousins." It turned out to be the truth. His mother had told him so. After that, we kind of made up. We even played together one day when Momma washed the meanest old lady's sheets at the house of Billy Joe's mother, my Aunt Mary, who owned a washing machine with a roller and a crank, because she had a dozen kids plus a husband.

Neither did the other surprise sneak up on me like a rabbit out of the bushes; I could see it coming a mile off. On that Friday of my lone week back at Hubbard Elementary, my teacher dispatched our final report cards for the year home with us.

"You children be so careful with your report cards," she announced from the front of our classroom, a portrait of George Washington, gazing over her shoulder. "I'm making you responsible. I know you can be little grownups when you take a notion. So make your mommies proud of you. When they see your grades for this year, they'll want to hug you. I know I do."

Like a little grownup I tried to lose my card on the way home, but I knew if I left it in the bushes Momma would promise me a switching and send me back looking for it. My card had a row of red check marks like a bunch of chinch bugs chasing each other, and my teacher's name in black. My card mostly reported a roll call of days absent. It also reported I'd failed the second grade.

The next morning I forgot about my failure. I was too excited about the adventure my mother and I were about to set out on. We planned to take the Greyhound bus and travel over to Corsicana and never see the old lady again in our lives. The wicked old woman sat hunched over in her rocking chair and sulked all the time we ate toast and jelly for our final breakfast. Never ever did she put Post Toasties or Grape Nuts on the table. This morning she was mad at Momma for leaving her "to the buzzards," as she put it, meaning her two sons that never wanted to visit her except to beg for something.

She was so mean at breakfast she made me turn off the radio which was telling about some soldiers over the water who'd got trapped by Germans and had to go home in boats. It didn't make sense to me, but they didn't mention any bombers, so I was interested in the soldiers. When she grumbled at me, "Turn off that racket before the battery goes down," it got into my mind that she might be a German spy.

After breakfast Momma put on her glasses and her coat, took me in one hand and our Woolworth suitcase in the other, and we left the old lady just sitting there in her rocking chair and walked downtown to catch the Greyhound when it stopped in the middle of the street. The whole business was new to me.

"Momma, what's it like to ride a Greyhound?"

"I ain't done it before, Baby, but I expect it's like riding in a big car."

"I'd like to see it go really fast," I said.

My mother laughed. "Well, I never seen a greyhound that run slow."

We were downtown ahead of the Greyhound, so Momma carried our suitcase into the Jones Brothers store where we sat on a wooden bench to wait for it. Nobody bothered us, since that was what the bench was for. The store had all kinds of groceries and cold drinks and cookies on shelves, which I looked at.

"How long does it take us to get to that town we're going to on the Greyhound?"

"I think about two hours maybe," said my mother.

"Maybe I should get something to eat on the way," I said. "I don't want people to see me with a headache when I get there."

From her purse my mother took a dime and a nickel and handed the coins to me.

"I expect you're right, Baby," she said. She watched me go over to the cookies stand.

That explains how I come to eat my first-ever box of Hi Ho crackers on my first-ever ride on the Greyhound. I'd picked out a box of Ritz crackers from the shelf, but Momma said Hi Hos were cheaper, only a dime, so I was eating them. And I sure loved that old Greyhound. I thought it resembled a huge blue and white loaf of Mrs. Baird's bread on wheels, and it had that picture of a stretched out greyhound on its side, running like its life depended on it getting somewhere.

Summer was coming on, the May weather had turned dry and balmy, so when the driver strolled along the aisle of the bus selling tickets, he lowered some of the windows, making it just right for me to crunch Hi Hos and sit in a breeze and watch fields and telephone poles rush behind us as we traveled. You could see plowed rows disappearing into the distance. Sometimes there'd be red and white cows way off in the fields and they seemed to move away from us as we sped along. I was sure I'd never gone that fast in my life, and the wind crazily whipped my hair if I laid my head on the window's ledge.

"Keep your head out of that window, Leon," Momma warned, "Them telephone poles wouldn't like nothing better than to knock you in the head."

When Momma and me stepped off the Greyhound in downtown Corsicana with our suitcase, there was a man waiting for us in a Plymouth automobile. Right away, that fancy car made my eyes bug out, mainly because most people I knew drove Model-A Fords, some of them old as I was. The Plymouth had a toy-like silver sailing ship poking right off the front of its hood. It looked snooty to me. The man wore a suit like you'd see in the Sears catalog. Later on, in private, Momma told me he was in insurance, which was alright with me.

It turned out the man was married to the lady who was in the hospital right then having a baby. I learned on the way to his house in the Plymouth that whatever it turned out to be, they'd bring it home and test it on their other two kids, then put Momma to work taking care of it.

The man's house was as snooty as his car, though all the houses along that street looked pretty much alike: white houses, front porches, cement steps, green grass, and sidewalks along the street. He drove the Plymouth up on a gravel driveway that seemed to go beyond the house to a garage. All told, this was more house than I'd ever had anything to do with.

The inside of the house was so full of marvels I couldn't have counted them on the fingers of both hands. Instead of cracky linoleum on the floors like I was used to, there was frizzy carpeting on every floor except the kitchen, which was bare wood but with soft rugs here and there. Every day my mother had to run a cleaning machine over the carpets, which looked like fun but was not, she said. By this time in my life, I'd lived with electric lights in our piece of a house back in Hubbard, but in this house there were lights on poles just standing around in nearly every corner. I liked it on days the kids were in school and I sat under the lights on poles and read Batman. When I read at home, I'd sit on wooden chairs that leaned one way or another; the chairs in this house were big and roomy, full of so much soft stuffing you could fall asleep in them without hurting yourself.

But there was no room in the house, not even the kitchen with its electric ice box, to compare with the bathroom. Of course, I, who was on an adventure, being now a few days short of eight years old, had never gone to the toilet without first going outside the house. Here, in this bathroom, you could go to the toilet or take a bath and never leave the room. You could go in the bathroom, lock the door, stand on a fluffy pink rug, take your clothes off, look at yourself in the wide mirror near the wash basin, sit on the deliciously shiny commode and pee, splash tap water into a grownup's tub, and bathe your body. And you could do all that twice a day if you dared, if your mother didn't want to know what you were up to. From time to time I just sat in the bathroom and thought about everything, even if it made me cry.

On that first day when we arrived in the house, I guess I looked like I'd never been away from home, standing inside the front room feeling bashful in front of all that furniture, while Mr. Thompson, that was his name, showed Momma around the house, let her know which would be our room and she could unpack our belongings in there. Then they came back in the front room and stood near me while he rattled his Plymouth car keys in his hands.

"We're sure glad you could come and help out, Aunt Bill," said Mr. Thompson, "I know I am. And Lucinda's going to need all the help you can give her when she gets home. The doctor said she needs to stay in bed for several days." He looked at me standing there holding an empty Hi Ho cracker box, and motioned at the door to the kitchen. "You and Leon go ahead and get yourselves some dinner, make yourselves at home. I'll drop by my office, and get the kids from school on my way home. I may want you to help me get Lucinda home Friday, and Leon can stay here at the house with Willdee and Dale if that's alright with you." Then Mr. Thompson left to go and sell some of his insurance and what'all.

My mother and me helped ourselves to some baloney and light-bread sandwiches in the kitchen, and got a Coca Cola from a big Frigidaire that hummed in one corner.

"Momma, are Mr. Thompson's kids the kind that don't have good minds?"

"I never heard of it," my mother said. "What makes you think so?"

"Because they're still in school and I'm out," I said. "Maybe it takes them longer to learn anything." I took another slice of baloney from a plate and put it on my light-bread and licked drippings of salad dressing off my fingers. "I don't think I can put up with people not in their right minds."

"Well, I expect their school runs longer here in a big city."

We finished our dinner and Momma cleaned up the table and washed our dishes. After the kitchen was clean, she set me down on a stuffed divan in the living room and gave me a telling off. I thought she was afraid I was about to lose my manners while she couldn't keep an eye on me in this big house with a baby on the loose.

"Leon, you listen to me, honey." She wasn't mad or anything, but she had on her serious face, looking through her glasses. "We got to stay here until Lucinda gets up with her baby. These kids will stay out of the way, and you'all can play." She put an arm around my shoulder to give me a hug, and kept it there, and looked around the room, as if she was studying to buy it. "I always wisht we'd had pretty furnishings like this."

There was a sadness in her voice like she might cry, which made me think she might be getting ready to carry on, so I got the subject changed right away. I moved over and sat in one of the stuffed chairs, just to try it out. There was something I'd been thinking about.

"Boy, it tickled me when I learned Billy Joe was kin to me," I said. "How many cousins do you figure I have somewheres?"

"Lord, I wish you hadn't mentioned it," she said. "Now I have to think about us going down to Union High and living with all that mess." She shook her head, and laughed, and I knew she wasn't going to carry on.

"What mess you talking about, Momma?"

"Sis and Wylie and all them kids," she said, and started to laugh like she'd hit her funny bone on the door post.

I didn't understand what she was laughing about, but I couldn't ask her then. We heard Mr. Thompson's car coming up his gravel driveway.

The front door busted open as if Mr. Thompson had drove his Plymouth into his own living room. Flinging book satchels and lunch boxes in two or three directions, his two kids chased each other through the door, screaming, "Leon! Leon! Where are you?" Both of them saw me, sitting froze to the stuffed chair, charged over to me, pushing and shoving each other so dangerously I thought maybe I was right about them not having good minds.

Willdee, shoulder to shoulder with me, might have been ten pounds heavier due to more food on his table; Dale was a touch smaller, but she was a girl anyway. I noticed Willdee wore pants to school, unlike me going all over creation in overalls. His sister had yellow curls which I thought would look better cut off, and wore a jumper over a dress, causing me to wonder if she was in the second grade, not that it made any difference, as far as I could see. But both of them were grabbing at me as if I was some kind of new pet.

Then Willdee did something that made him my best friend for the next two weeks.

"Come on, Leon," he shouted, grabbing me by an arm. "Let's go listen to the Tom Mix Straight Shooters on the radio."

There in their living room, against the wall near a corner lamp, stood the grandest radio I'd ever seen. It was a Zenith console, wide as an ice box, decorated with figured cloth over round places where the voices came out, and furnished near the top with knobs and dials for picking out the radio programs. A light stood on and let you see a needle move across the radio stations all over the world as you twisted the knobs. The radio was taller than Willdee, and it hypmotized me completely. I'd be under its power the rest of my life, I reckoned.

Tom Mix rode his famous horse Tony out of that radio, directly from station WRR in Dallas, and into the Thompson's living room every day soon as Willdee got home from school. I'd be holding my breath until both of us piled down on the floor in front of the radio, didn't even need chairs, just laid on our stomachs. First, you'd hear Tony galloping fast as hoofs could pound. Then, Tom Mix couldn't wait to get there, and he'd shout, "Dig dirt, Tony." You knew no bandit or outlaw'd ever escape in whatever episode you'd listen to. One day it might be an evil gang of penitentiary escapees who hated Tom Mix for putting them on the rock pile; the next day it might be a dishonest sheriff who feared Tom Mix would find out he had bamboozled a banker. But they all had to face Tom Mix and his guns.

After a few days I knew any boy could become a Ralston Straight Shooter of America by eating his breakfast cereal out of a red-and-white checkered box and mailing in the boxtop for his own fingerprinting identification card. Willdee helped me mail off my box top, but I'd gone by the time it arrived in his mailbox, and I never got to be a Straight Shooter until years afterwards. I guess because I was pretty expert about cowboys from reading *Broncho Bill* a million times, that while I listened to the radio I could see a picture of Tom Mix in my head or somewhere: a broad-brimmed white hat, a red and yellow shirt with darts for pockets, almost knee-high cowboy boots, two silvery six-shooters in his holsters, and a smart horse, Tony. I wasn't sure about his face, but was sure I'd have no trouble recognizing him if we ran into each other one day.

Listening to Tom Mix was the first, but not the only one of the adventures Willdee and I shared during mine and Momma's stay in his house. It was like that boy ran on an electric battery, never standing in one place longer than it took to eat a bowl of Ralston's whole wheat cereal, every day thinking up excitements I considered dangerous. Dale, of course, never bothered us unless she juned around in some awful way. Once she wanted us to put on a circus, a project that gathered several kitchen chairs and a table cloth in the back yard before my mother came looking for the missing table cloth. I never could keep up with what Dale did all day, me and her brother being as busy as we were. But I guess the grandest adventure Willdee and I shared was the one featuring the gang of "claim jumpers." At least, it was the adventure I learned the most from.

I soon found out Willdee had a running feud with some boys who often played along a railroad track that ran beyond a vacant lot behind the Thompson's back yard. He showed them to me one day at a considerable distance, three or four rough-looking boys, all dragging sticks along the railroad ties, making clacking noises. Those boys must have lived in run-down houses, and considered the tracks to be their rightful playground, for they trolled behind trains that came through, chunked rocks at bottles, and walked on the rails. Willdee considered them to be "claim jumpers," as he told me. His usual practice was to sneak behind a board fence on the other side of the railroad tracks and discharge a flurry of rocks at the boys, then dash home and into the house.

"I've got a good idea how we can get rid of those claim jumpers, Leon."

Armed with the least possible knowledge about "claim jumpers," plus hearsay about this gang of jumpers, I was nevertheless proud that Willdee included me in his invasion plans. I was in a mood for all the excitement I could get, even if I learned something, too.

"Tell me about my part," I said.

"Ammunition is first important," said Willdee, holding up a rock the size of his fist.

According to his plan, we'd collect as many rocks as we could carry at one time. He'd hide behind the fence as he usually did. My part was to walk up the track toward the boys, then catch their attention by throwing as many rocks as I could really fast. When they chased me, he'd counterattack from his fence line with his load of fist-sized rocks. They'd never know what hit them. I pictured it in my mind. I imagined them running like cowards. The plan looked dandy for the most part.

"Won't I have to be pretty close before I can hit them with my rocks?" I was worried if I could surprise them before they spotted me.

"They're so dumb they may just think you're a railroad tramp," he explained. "We see them all the time back here on the tracks, catching trains going by. These claim jumpers won't know what hit 'em."

Because Willdee wore pants instead of "overhauls" like me, he poked so many rocks in his pockets that his pockets stuck out funny. I figured he didn't plan on running much. Plus, he had rocks in both hands. I loaded up with all I could carry in my hands, juggling without dropping them.

I wasn't sure what tramps looked like, though I couldn't believe they carried a bunch of rocks every place they went looking for a train. But I so much looked forward to seeing Willdee jump out from the back of his fence, heaving his rocks, I began to saunter along between the tracks as if I was waiting for a train to come through going to Dallas.

Three boys were along the tracks, maybe fifteen yards from me, whaling daylights out of a cardboard box they'd found. Whack! Whack! Whack! They were so busy no one spied me until I was up close enough to chunk my first rock. It hit one boy on the leg and must have smarted, for he dropped his stick, forgot the box, and yelped. His buddies stopped whacking the box, looked first at him, then saw me about the time I flung my second rock. It missed everybody and tumbled among the railroad ties.

"Hey, you'all stop that!" The biggest boy, maybe their leader, shouted at me.

I threw my last rock, which skipped against an iron rail, causing a humming sound along the rail. It came to rest near the boy I'd hit, and he grabbed it up and furiously cast it back at me, but he was in a hurry and the rock went high and wide. Then was when I started to run.

Pretty much at once I learned it's not easy running across railroad ties.

"It's that damn Willdee!" I heard one boy shout behind me, apparently so used to him throwing rocks they couldn't accept anyone else as rock thrower.

Rocks clattered around me as I stumbled over the ties, intensely aware of boys running back of me, mad as dirt daubers. A few more feet along, and I passed the end of the board fence. One good-sized stone ricocheted off the boards and tumbled ahead of me.

Suddenly Willdee sprang from behind the fence, loaded down with rocks.

"Hey!" He screamed at the running "claim jumpers," and began flinging rocks at them before they could come to a halt. They must have been not only surprised, but also dumbfounded. Where did this second Willdee come from?

"God-dang his hide!" One jumper was clearly beaned with one of Willdee's rocks, for he was the one who yelled, but he recovered the rock that hit him and returned it at its thrower, who tried to get behind the fence again. But he was so weighted with rocks he couldn't move quickly, and I heard more rocks hitting the fence, then Willdee shouted "Hey!" again, and I turned in time to see a rock bounce off his head.

Probably the sight of blood brought the battle to an end. Blood oozed off Willdee's scalp, ran over one eye, and trickled onto his cheek. He began to yell and cry. The three claim jumpers, holding unlaunched rocks in their hands, stood frozen, watching this bloody drama. I watched the excitement from a safe distance, as I had no rocks left. Finally, the leader of the boys spoke up.

"You lucky you didn't lose no eye, Willdee," he said.

Back at the house Momma about dropped her ironing when Willdee entered the kitchen screaming and yelling and bloody as a pirate. His own mother even got out of bed and came in the kitchen to see him dying. I never found out what the new baby thought about the racket since he stayed shut up for once. Dale ran into the kitchen to observe the saving of Willdee's life.

"Maybe he'll have a big scar," she said hopefully.

The bleeding stopped right away when Momma put a wet cloth on Willdee's noggin. Even his momma breathed the sigh of relief. And I guess we all thought that was the end of that.

But it wasn't.

The following Sunday, the third of June, 1940, was my eighth birthday. It was a few days later I learned on the Zenith radio that my birthday was the first day the German Luftwaffe had bombed Paris over the water somewheres. It was scary thinking the Germans were getting close-by. But more immediate to my life was a birthday cake on the front porch of the Thompson's own house. I don't remember receiving a birthday gift, for gifts in my family were reserved for the

Christmas season. But Momma baked me a cake, and all of us, even Mr. Thompson's wife and the new baby in a dress, sat on the porch and ate cake with candles on it. We had a good time, except for the baby who cried and had its smelly diapers changed. The day itself was sunny, plenty warm on the porch, no clouds in the sky, and I was happy that I'd gone another year older.

Willdee and I finished our cake and went onto their lawn to play with his set of four new horseshoes, manufactured so you could pitch them at a stake you drove in the ground with a hammer. Dale stayed on the porch because of the new dress she was wearing. About the first horseshoe we pitched we saw him coming, the biggest of the murderous claim jumpers. He looked dressed for Sunday School, but still tough even though he was wearing a cap and whipcord pants. His path would take him directly along the sidewalk in front of the Thompson's house.

"Come on, Leon, let's get on the porch with Daddy and them until he goes past."

The porch had a railing about waist high. Willdee and I stood behind the railing to watch the claim jumper walk past, a genuine entertainment. I held my breath when he got right in front of the porch, afraid to look directly at him. That's when Willdee called out, "Who said you could use our sidewalk?"

Willdee's voice scared me enough that I jumped and let out my breath. What in the world, I thought. The claim jumper must have thought so, too, for he stopped and looked at us up there on the porch. Then he walked right up the cement walk to the porch steps and never took off his cap. Nobody on the porch said a word and they were grownups. Either the boy wasn't scared or he thought right was on his side. He could have walked up the porch steps. Instead, he balled up his fists, raised them up like a prize fighter I saw once in *Tip Top* comics, and spoke directly at me.

"Come down here, coward, so's I can knock your block off."

I came close to peeing in my pants until I realized he was looking past me at Willdee.

Of course, Willdee didn't go down there to get his block knocked off. From what I could see, he stayed backed up against the screen door while the claim jumper punched the air and danced around right on Mr. Thompson's lawn. Somewhere I'd read about a whirling dervish. The boy was it. He pushed over the horseshoe stake. Then he walked off and went on down the sidewalk. The baby started shrieking and Mr. and Mrs. Thompson took it inside the house. Dale went in after them. Momma took my birthday cake with eight candles in the house. That left two of us on the porch. I stayed put until Willdee moved to the porch railing and stood beside me.

"Happy birthday, Leon," he said.

One morning all I could find to do was sit on the porch in the nice, warm Texas morning sunshine and think. Cars once in a while rolled past in the street. Nobody paid the least attention to me sitting on the porch, my bare feet resting on the steps. Lately the June bugs had begun to chatter in the trees, about making your ears ring if you paid attention to them. But on this day the sun warmed me, and I partly napped and partly worried about Momma and me going to live in that "mess" at Union High. Today I felt like I should give such things some thought. I knew we'd have to move soon. I give thought to how many times we'd moved since Daddy died. It didn't seem like any place was home anymore, which made me wonder how I'd ever get out of the second grade if I didn't have a home. Maybe I was stuck there forever.

In the kitchen Momma was making a banana pudding for us to have at supper. The table was laid out with bananas, vanilla wafers, and cans of Carnation condensed milk. I guessed Mrs. Thompson was learning how to make banana pudding, because it is so good. She and the baby were pulled up to the table where she could watch my mother, and the baby just looked goggle-eyed. I begged a vanilla wafer and tried not to look at the ugly baby.

"Can I do something?" I asked.

I didn't know that I was getting ready to go get dog bit.

"I reckon you can," said my mother. "I ain't got but one hen's egg for the pudding. What I want you to do is, you go down the street to that house with the big tree in the yard. It's a neighbor lives there, and she will lend you an egg if you ask her." Momma reached underneath the table and brought up an empty milk bottle. "While you're there, thank her for this bottle of milk she sent Lucinda for the baby."

I took the bottle and wandered down the street looking for a big tree.

When I got to the yard in front of the neighbor's, there was a little old black and white dog about the size of a mailbox sitting on the porch. It was a short haired dog that looked like it hoped to grow up one day. As soon as I walked underneath the big tree and stepped onto the lawn, the little dog jumped to its feet and began to bark like I was a robber. Since I'd never had any trouble with dogs before, I said "howdy" and "nice dog," and kept on walking up on the lawn. The dog jumped off the porch and hopped forward on stiff legs, barking and showing its teeth, which made me nervous.

Then I thought of my milk bottle and raised it up like a club.

"Git back, you dog, or I'll smack you a good'un," I shouted.

The dog dashed at me, and I swung the bottle. I missed, and the dog grabbed my ankle with his sharp little teeth, and I slung him off. I dropped my bottle and ran back to the street. By the time I got to the house, my ankle was bleeding. I yelped for help when I got on the porch, but I didn't cry. I was fascinated by the thought of being bit by a dog, which I'd never done before. I noticed I had little blue puncture marks on my ankle. It looked like I'd entered a new stage in life, and I figured I was ready to face the "mess" down there at Union High which Momma had mentioned but not explained to me. Maybe I'd never get out of the second grade, but I'd survived a dog attack.

Chapter 8

A MESS OF COUSINS

It dawned on me that morning in Corsicana that every time I got into a car I was going somewhere. I knew that some people joy-rode around in cars, kind of looking at buildings or the clothes on folks walking on the streets, enjoying the view, then went home to supper. But every time I stepped into one, and made myself comfortable, the car headed for a certain place, where I'd have to get out and stay there. For me, a car was a kind of delivery truck. Probably the thought come to me that day because Mr. Thompson's new Plymouth automobile was so nice and comfortable. It glided easily along the streets, its toy-ship hood ornament pointing the way, and inside the car the fuzzy upholstery was soft to the touch and gave off a new-car smell so smart that I'd liked to have rode around breathing it, looked at the sights in the big city of Corsicana, then returned to Mr. Thompson's house to eat our supper of fried chicken at his dining table. But the Plymouth was taking us to the Greyhound station. I knew I'd be "dumped out" with Momma and be sent along to the little town of Dawson where we'd be met by Mr. Waller and Uncle Wylie. We were going to live in the "mess" Momma had laughed about, but not explained to me yet.

It had taken only two weeks in Corsicana to transform me, a jug-eared kid from the country, a reader of funny books, into a high-toned city boy. Fourteen days of indoor plumbing, warm baths in a porcelain tub, a refrigerated icebox full of baloney, the Zenith radio full of the adventures of Tom Mix, and supper at a polished dining table loaded with napkins had created in me a taste for high-toned living. I couldn't foresee that my city-street life was preparing to dogleg onto the crooked, narrow road to the cotton patch.

Before we boarded that blue-and-white Greyhound again, Momma bought me a five-cent Baby Ruth candy bar in the bus station, and I tried to make it last all the way to Dawson by pinching peanuts off the caramel to eat them slowly. But the June sun beat in the windows and the bus heated up even with the windows rolled down, and the chocolate melted on my hands until Momma complained so I had to go ahead and eat it. Left without anything to do but read a Batman comic book I'd read a million times, I began to worry about the "mess" we were headed into.

"Momma, tell me about the mess down there at Union High," I said. "It worries me so much I can't think straight."

It was plain for me to see that my mother was worried also. She'd wanted to sit beside the open window, and she wasn't talking much, keeping to herself behind a serious face, gazing out the window at the passing scenery. Even her hair looked severe. She'd got her hair trimmed short the day before we left Corsicana, as though nobody knew how to cut hair where we were going. Studying her face, I realized Momma never used lipstick like that Mrs Thompson spread on her lips, or the black paint she used on her eyebrows. I guessed it didn't make any difference to Momma how she looked.

"Oh, Baby, I was pulling your calf-rope about the mess, knowing you don't have no idea how many of them cousins there are." She wasn't joking now, but thoughtful, probably like she wondered how in the world I'd get along with a mess of cousins. "All I meant was they's a mess of kids at Sis and Wylie's place," she went on. "I don't think you've played with them more than a time or two. You'll have to get along with them, so don't get all swole up, you hear me?" Now it was looking like I might be the one to cause trouble, not the mess.

She held her hands up and began to count on her fingers. "Katie, Gladys, Bootsie, and Betty, that makes four for Sis. Then Ett's got Frankie, Deanna, and Sammie, which makes seven in all." She paused and thought, and said, "Since Bud's living with them, I expect there'll be Melvin Junior, too." All the fingers she had left were thumbs.

"You mean I got to live with eight cousins I don't know a thing about?" I was near struck dumb, never having been told anything so unheard of. It made me remember something I'd seen in a comic book, about some place over the water where people went around all day wearing bones in their noses, and you could believe it or not, but it was true as everything. Now I was going to be a believe-it-or-not kid, except they probably wouldn't let me wear a bone in my nose. While the bus rolled along, I rode silently the rest of the way to Dawson, counting cousins off on both my hands. Katie, Gladys, Frankie....

There they were, Mr. Waller and Uncle Wylie, waiting for us when the Greyhound edged into the curb in Dawson, a small town along one lonely street from all I could see. There were a couple of wooden benches on the shady part of the street, set against the building where we had parked, one bench occupied by three white men wearing overalls and straw hats, their legs crossed at the knees, looking to be farmers in town for the day, passing the news. On the other bench sat a black man, and a black woman who had a suitcase with her as if she was going away on the Greyhound. The black woman had a little boy with her, but he didn't have any Baby Ruth. I saw he was trying to take a peek at me, but I didn't care. I must have looked a sight to the little black kid. I gave him a wink, but he hid behind his momma. My grandfather came up to us and put Momma and me and our suitcase in the back seat of Wylie's Model-A Ford, and we set off for Union High, wherever in the wide world it might be since nobody told me.

Uncle Wylie drove, one arm resting on his window, and told us how glad he was that we'd come on down to live with the family. I liked Uncle Wylie right off, a jolly man with a slight limp, who laughed easily and didn't treat me like an orphan or a piece of furniture, but talked to me man-to-man. Of course, Mr. Waller ignored me, sputtered at my mother, and cussed like a banty rooster, and spat snuff juice out his window, so little streaks of brown appeared and disappeared along the outside of my window. He fussed at my mother for leaving her furniture up there in Hubbard. It was like he was going to run her life for her. I wondered if that would be a "mess."

The car took us through country that didn't look like much to me, nothing to catch your eye except level fields that would probably turn into cotton patches in the heat of the summer, not that it wasn't already hot enough to cook a egg. It struck me as I watched the fields roll past the car window that we were entering a new country, for the fields were so level and large, just going on forever, even more so than at Mr. David's. Maybe, I thought, I'm just starting to notice fields, and I wondered if I'd have to look across this country of Union High until I was sick of it. After we rode along a country road through the cotton fields, stirring up dust clouds behind us, for what seemed about eight or ten miles, Uncle Wylie pulled the car into a gasoline station where two farm roads crossed.

The station had two gas pumps with round globes on top painted with the word "Texaco." A kind of porch stuck off a small plank building behind the pumps, a store, I guessed, because it had a screen door with tin "Rainbow Bread" banners on it and a window that somebody had stuck a sign on it advertising "Dr Pepper, Ten, Two, and Four." Next to the door was a red, tin cooler for soda pop that I imagined contained some of those Dr Peppers floating in icy water, and my mouth seemed dry enough that I could have drunk two of them right there. The porch made some shade in the hot noon-day sunshine, and two old men set on rickety chairs out of the sun. I'd bet those chairs were there every day, starting with George Washington. Both men leaned back like they thought they owned the country. I couldn't see much else here, maybe a cotton gin off in back of the gas station. Wylie and Mr. Waller got out of the car and walked toward the old men in their chairs. They all seemed to know each other and said "howdy."

"I wish we'd hurry up and get to that old Union High," I said mostly to myself, looking out the window past Momma at the

"Texaco" globes. "It's hot as a oven in this car." I felt sweat leak out of my hair.

My mother wiped sweat off my neck with her handkerchief.

"Baby, this *is* Union High," she said softly, as if she couldn't make herself say it.

My brain stuck like a tractor axle-deep in mud. It couldn't calculate together two Texaco pumps, a country store selling Rainbow Bread, a cotton gin, and two old men chewing tobacco, and come up with a Union High. What my mind finally told me was if I had to trade a Plymouth automobile and a big white house in Corsicana for Union High, the only thing to do was cry. And I did. I cried until Momma said we didn't have no choice, so hush up and think about something else. That's when I started to wonder where those eight cousins, the "mess," hid out. I was expecting to be picked on.

My first impression of Union High was pretty accurate. As Momma said, "It was a wide place in the road, that's all." As I was to find out, the little country store was the center of about everything, considering there was also a church, the cotton gin, a cemetery, a bunch of ancient houses, and two schools, one for lower grades, a smaller one for upper grades. I would learn the history of Union High later on in the grade school, that it had been settled way back, all the way in the last century, and it sat on a crossroads of two Farm-to-Market roads, 638 and 642, placing us eight miles from the nearest "real" town, Dawson, all of us stuck way off in Navarro County.

My struggle to hush up crying was interrupted by Mr. Waller and Wylie returning to the car. Mr. Waller told Momma that some man was going to loan him and Wylie a truck on the weekend so they'd go up to Hubbard and get her bed and kitchen stuff and bring it all down to Wylie's house.

Uncle Wylie had lit up a roll-your-own cigarette right out of a Bull Durham tobacco sack, and it hung off his lip as if he was eating it. He started up the car, and we rolled off.

"House is just a ways along here," he said, as we continued on the road we came in on. "That mess of young'uns is layin' for you, Leon. You better get ready to run." Wylie looked at me in the dashboard mirror, winked, and laughed out cigarette smoke. Because he seemed like a nice man, I felt like he was joking about me getting ready to run. Except that had already took up in my mind.

No sooner than we had started, he pulled the car into the yard of a house that squatted on the bare ground like it had given up trying to stand a long time ago. It kind of reminded me of the house on Mr. David's place where I was born; it was all weather-worn unpainted planks and had a front porch that struggled to support its shingled overhang with upright wood posts. Only this house had more holes in it than I was used to, missing planks here and there, shingles blown off, cracks in the porch you could step through in the dark, and vacant widow panes. To me, the old house sure didn't look like anybody's home.

The "mess" of kids arranged on the porch, some leaning on posts, a couple sitting on the steps, one or two in the shade holding smaller ones, called to my mind a faded black-and-white photograph I'd seen in a magazine of a bunch of outlaws in the old West laying about in their hideout. Robber's Roost. I knew at once these robbers were laying for me. But the first lesson I learned at Union High was: cousins are a kid's best friend. Melvin Junior, the red-haired cousin, stood off the front stoop, motioned to me, and shouted, "Come on in the house, Big Ears!"

Melvin Junior was the oldest cousin, two years older than I was, and bigger than any of us. He even got to wear cord pants and a belt instead of overalls. He had freckles and fierce red hair, which got him called "Red" at school, the most risky name around. The oldest girl was Katie Ruth, her age falling between Melvin's and mine. Katie got good grades in school, and was a mature guide for the younger kids, worked hard to help around the house, and always laughing. She had the nicest freckles. Next biggest was Frankie, two years below me, a small kid, who wore his hair any way he'd like, also in overalls. Frankie was more or less trapped between Melvin and me. He was easy to pick on and be plotted against by both of us if he was needed for a dangerous scheme, then he could get his bottom spanked by Aunt Ett. Finally, Gladys was the oldest of the "little kids," already in school and wearing glasses, perched on a nose that set right smack in the middle of a field of freckles, where Bootsie, Deana, Betty Sue, and Sammie were still too young to attend. In this scale of things, I had become the new kid, the ninth cousin, when I counted them off on my fingers. What this all meant to me, of course, was that I was now in this tribe of cousins to stay. Union High was now going to be my home for the rest of my born life, like it or not, and I wasn't quite sure how I felt about that.

Cousins, of course, come with aunts and uncles. I hadn't seen Uncle Bud, my mother's brother, but only a few times, I guess, because I didn't remember him well. He had moved away from Mr. Hickman's after his wife died with the pneumonia, and she was buried in the cemetery at Cottonwood in the dead of the worst winter in history, her coffin being moved in a wagon with mules. Melvin Junior had moved with his daddy. I learned to like Uncle Bud because, though he was one of the hardest-working and most responsible members of the family, he was also full of jokes and tricks, a kind of grownup kid himself, inside, though he'd had to drop out of school in the third grade to work in the fields with Mr. Waller.

"Leon, what's your middle name," Uncle Bud would ask in some situation.

"It's Leon," I'd answer, wondering why he'd ask such a dumb question.

"No, it ain't," he'd respond. "Your middle name is Mud if I have to ask you one more time to stop reading funny books." And he'd laugh, because I'd fallen for the same joke a million times before.

Aunt Sis was my mother's youngest sister, and Katie's mother, and married to Uncle Wylie. She was a pretty woman with dark hair and a pleasant manner, looking a bit like my own mother except Aunt Sis had brown hair, always calm as if nothing rattled her. Sis ran the family and kept things together. My Aunt Ett, sort of like Momma, wore her red hair short, and she was short, and her temper went along with that, maybe because her life had been some more troubled than her sisters' lives. She would sometimes give Frankie a spanking if he got out of sorts, so she was a bit more dangerous for us roughneck kids.

Momma and me were given a room off to one side of the front room, where Momma's dresser, quilt box, and trunk come to rest when the truck arrived back from Hubbard. I was glad to see the trunk, for I knew it contained valuable stuff: my strip of India rubber, Daddy's pocket knife, most of my comic books, and Momma's tobacco sack of dimes, her backup against total disaster. She sorted these new belongings in with Aunt Sis's furniture, and put Daddy's picture on her dresser, reminding me that sooner or later she would carry on again. To tell the truth, I was near about to carry on myself and would have if Melvin Junior and Frankie had not been watching every move I'd made since I'd come in the old house.

Because the house itself extended back further than it appeared from the front yard, there were several bed rooms and a kitchen, plus a hallway, though the house had no bathroom with frizzy rugs on the floor and a big mirror where you could stand naked and look at yourself. And the toilet was out back where everyone had to take turns. Of course, there was no Zenith radio, no Frigidaire full of ice cubes and baloney, and no carpet cleaning machine. I looked around the place and was overwhelmed with the thought that if this old house with holes in it, here in the Union High, was home, then I was back where I started. My eight-year-old brain had been unceremoniously crammed with images of a high-toned way of living with Dale and Willdee up there in Corsicana until it near about deceived me to think that was real life.

But now high-tone had got up and left and wasn't coming back.

Chapter 9

THE BIRTH OF CONSCIENCE

The last thing I wanted to truck with in the steamy summer of 1940 was a work ethic. By the end of June and the beginning of July in Texas, any year, the "heat of the day" makes its move on the field worker by dinner time at noon, then, with the sun overhead, multiplies degrees of heat throughout the afternoon, reaching a blistering hundred-plus temperature before you can say the words "heat stroke." Maybe I *was* only eight years old, going on nine, but I'd seen enough work in the fields at Mr. David's to know I didn't want to actually *do* any part of it. And, of course, my two weeks of leisure living as a city boy in Corsicana hadn't done anything to prepare me for the reality of life on a cotton farm in way-off Navarro County. Not yet nine, though, I now reluctantly found myself face to face with the realism of my situation. It was my time to be stood up against the wall of hard labor by the person who'd been on both sides of the firing line: my mother.

I discovered my fateful doom one day when Momma stood me on a piece of white paper in my socks and traced a pencil stub around my feet. It looked to me like she'd traced two fat, wobbly snow men on the paper when she finished. She took the piece of paper and folded it with an order form from the Sears catalog, and put the papers into an envelope. Because I liked going to the mail box and finding packages from the catalogs, I asked her if she'd ordered a surprise for me.

"Ordering you a pair of shoes, Baby," she said.

That sounded good, as my high-top tennis shoes were faded, worn, and getting tight on my growing feet. I wanted to see what kind of new shoes I was going to have.

"I hope they're cowboy boots, Momma," I said. "I wear cowboy boots, I'll look like Broncho Bill." Boy, I couldn't wait!

My mother hauled the Sears catalog up on her lap, turned a few pages, and pointed to my shoes she'd just ordered. A picture of them was underneath her finger. They were ankle-high brown leather shoes with thick rubber soles and blunt toes that bulged like knobs on a log. Round metal eyes holding shoe strings led up the front of the shoe from toe to ankle, where two hooks bent over to hold your knotted strings. They were the ugliest shoes I'd ever seen! Li'l Abner wore those shoes in the comics, and he was a hill billy!

"These are good work shoes," said Momma.

"They're ugly old shoes," I screamed, and started to cry. I was hoping for cowboy boots, and I was going to get clod-hoppers. "Besides, I can't work, because I don't know how." My disappointment so overwhelmed me that I didn't know what to do. "I just wish I was dead," I cried, and pushed the old catalog off her lap.

"Hush up, Leon," Momma said, "You ain't no Big Ike from Corsicana I can't tan you."

Momma didn't tan me after all, but she did carry on. She told me that we didn't have any money, just the little she got from staying with the Thompson's baby in Corsicana, not mentioning the dimes in the tobacco sack. Every penny we got, even if I got fifty cents hoeing in the fields, would keep us from starving, from being out on the roads like old hoboes, she said. But it was like she couldn't talk about us starving without her crying. I guess that's what made me feel bad about wanting the cowboy boots, so I stopped begging, didn't worry about a tanning. Momma's crying always left me helpless.

"Uncle Bud's found me a job up the road here a ways," Momma said, and wiped her eyes on her apron. "Cleaning house for some people, getting their breakfast on the table. It's just in the mornings, so I can do field work after dinner." She closed up the Sears catalog, and put her arm around my shoulder and hugged me. "I can't keep from crying to think of my baby having to go out in the cotton field, too." She took her glasses out of her apron pocket, and breathed on them and wiped them with the apron before putting them on. "Papa made us kids go to the fields little as you, and I said I'd never have a kid of mine out hoeing cotton like we done." She patted me on the cheek and got up and went off in another room with the Sears catalog, looking for a stamp to stick on the envelope.

Except for the dirt road running in front of our yard and some fenced pasture and a stock tank directly behind the house we lived in, we lived surrounded by cotton fields. On the other side of the fence, cows often gathered in the shade of an occasional tree and lazily chewed their cuds, swishing horseflies away with their tails, while a few hardy cows slowly grazed around the pasture hoping to find grass or weeds not burned dead yet. Beyond the pasture were a few shacks where black families lived, and you'd see little black kids playing in the yard, running around like any kids will do. In every other direction cotton rows paralleled into the distance.

I guess nobody who grows up in Texas cotton country ever forgets the landscape of a tidy cotton patch shimmering in July or August heat, the sun's rays forming mirages, and miniature whirlwinds making dustdevils dance over the rows. The same person will remember the hot, back-breaking labor that was required to keep those long, straight rows tidy. Cockleburrs, weeds, and Johnson grass viciously flourished in the same rich bottomland or blackland soil that sustained cotton plants, making the uprooting or chopping down of these undesirables necessary lest they starve the cotton. Plows and cultivators, whether pulled by mules or tractors, worked the fields as soon as little green shoots came up in the cotton beds. But the cruelest work, I learned early, was hoeing and chopping cotton, done by hand in order to clear weeds and thin the growing plants. Especially in the month of June a field could be pretty, if all you had to do was drive past in a new car and look at it and go on to the next town for a Coca Cola. Cotton blooms sprang open all over the patch in whites, reds, and browns, to drop off and be replaced as July heated up by dark green bolls in the shape of hard-boiled eggs. As the days of August dried out the fields, the bolls opened and revealed puffy locks of cotton.

Memories of the cotton patch prevail. On the June afternoon when Momma introduced me to hard labor in the cotton patch, there were still squares on the plants from which sprang white and red blossoms. I pulled some off, bunched them into a bouquet, but she told me to don't and that was that for playing. She'd told me I only had to work a half day, during the time she was in the field. Because the cutting edges of the hoes were filed sharp, an accident might happen if you fooled around, so Momma watched me to see I didn't chop a toe. I was given a crooked-neck hoe with a handle almost as long as a man was tall, but I was only tall as a post with a hat on, so I had to grip the handle in its middle, thus kept on whacking myself in the head with the tall end of it. Momma showed me how to chop weeds and grass along the sides of the bed and in the rows and leave the thinning of the plants to her. In my first attempts to hoe around the plants, I had chopped down too many of them. But I learned to chop along beside my mother, my hands sore and blistered before quitting time.

In looking back at this time in my life, I'm amazed that as an eight-year-old I didn't make more of a fuss for my mother about going to work every day in the heat and sweat of the cotton fields. Of course, I complained at first about minor things, like my ugly clodhopper shoes, and the straw hat I had to wear, sometimes chase it across the field when a breeze whipped it off my head. But Momma had said right away she wouldn't put up with no hissy fits, and had pulled up a cotton stalk for a threat. Even so, there was more to it than threats. To have her carry on was far worse for me than a switching. And, too, the immediate conditions of my life, of those of our neighbors, and of our family, all showed everyone laboring at life. As far as I could see, that's what people did, worked the land.

By the end of June nearly everyone in our family was strung out down those rows of cotton, hoes in hand, digging weeds up by their roots. Only a few of us didn't chop cotton. Uncle Bud and Uncle Wylie, experts with motors and big machines, drove tractors and cultivated fields where the cotton plants were smaller. Those kids who were younger than my age, like Frankie and Gladys, got to stay back at the house with Aunt Sis, the cook and house cleaner and kid watcher. So any time I stood upright and propped on my hoe handle, wiped sweat out of my eyes, and checked the sun's height in the sky to see how long it was until "quitting time," I could see, spread out across the rows at different intervals, my mother, Mr. Waller, Melvin Junior, Aunt Ett, and Katie. Also hoeing cotton with us were mothers and daddies and kids from the colored families who lived in the shacks beyond the pasture. Until I learned to work without hoeing down the plants or chopping off my foot, I worked beside my mother, but by the time blisters had popped and healed on my hands I was paired with Melvin Junior, who had already worked in the fields for a year. He and I were supposed to carry a row between us, working either side, and we'd get paid equal to one grownup if we behaved, not always the easiest thing to do.

Melvin Junior was a few inches taller than I was, showed off a million freckles across his nose, and he wore a red straw hat that looked like it had been sprayed with wax, curious because he had red hair. But my cousin did everything unlike other people as long as he could get away with it without Uncle Bud tanning him with a belt. He even hoed cotton barefooted, leading me to try it until I burned my feet in the hot sand and made Momma threaten me with a stalk of cotton.

"You cut your foot off with that hoe and I'd like to know where we'd be then, Leon," she yelled at me.

"I know where you'd be," said Melvin Junior behind Momma's back. "It'd be in the toilet where sissies get their baby toes." He laughed at me as I put my shoes back on.

"Bet I can cut your toes off and throw 'em down the toilet hole," I said, and poked my hoe at his bare feet, making him dance a jig.

"Leon," my mother was shouting now, "you and Melvin Junior quit that and pick up your row or I'm coming back there with a cotton stalk." In time I'd learn that she'd do that if we made her get mad enough. We'd have to get back to work, because she could also tell on Melvin Junior to Uncle Bud.

Most of the time me and him worked together without fur flying. Having somebody to talk and laugh with made the time go faster, relieved the drudgery of chopping up one row, then chopping down the next all through the afternoon.

It was a new thing for me to be so tired out in the evenings that I'd eat my supper of iced tea and cornbread and pinto beans, and then go out and lie like a dead and rotten body on the front porch. I looked up through the holes in the porch ceiling at the stars and listened while Bud and Wylie and Mr. Waller told stories and cussed tractors until time for bed. Usually, I was too tired to play after supper. Before my daddy'd died, I'd been too little to go to the fields, had spent my days playing or going to school. Then I'd lived in Hubbard with Momma, where I'd failed the second grade, but at least I'd had time to read comic books. So much of my time back then was free time, given over to a listless leisure without worries other than bullies like Billy Joe and periods of boredom in the presence of grownups. The real worries about where our next homes and meals came from had all been Momma's. Somewhere in the back of my tired mind there now lurked a suspicion that I was getting mixed up in grownup's worries before my time.

The dirt road in front of our house separated our yard from a cotton field that appeared to go ahead all the way to Navarro Creek. Traffic on the road, though sparse, had beat down the sand and clay into a hard surface not unlike a town's street except when it rained on winter days. Bar ditches ran along either side of the road, carrying run-off when it rained, collecting trash at other times. If you turned left out of the yard, you'd go until you reached the creek, then the road went uphill, passed a farmhouse, and kept on going out of sight. I never knew where it went. But if you turned right from our yard, it took you to the Union High crossroads, the location of the store, gas station, church, cotton gin, and storage sheds. And the schools were pretty much right there, too. When you thought about it, that road was Main Street, Union High. And during the year I lived there, every adventure, scrape, fright, and narrow escape I had took place on or near that road.

Melvin Junior was used to work and Frankie didn't have to, owing to his age, so it wasn't long before they began to pull me off the porch in the evenings. Sometimes after supper the three of us walked up the road to the store on errands for the grownups. Aunt Sis might need a loaf of Rainbow bread or Mr. Waller would give us a nickel if we'd get him a tin of Garrett's snuff, then we'd buy penny candy out of a glass jar in the store and divide it on the way back to the house. Of course, I can't be sure, but it's my guess that there's no place more fertile for growing mischief than in the minds of boys strolling along a dirt road after dark, eating Tootsie Rolls. It wasn't long, then, until

I was tough enough to swing a hoe all afternoon, and then ramble the road in the evenings on the lookout for fun.

One of the places me and Melvin Junior and Frankie, along with any other boys who lived close by, used for playing was a large storage shed, a kind of wooden crib for holding corn that the gin operators had located between the gin and the store. There were two rooms with high ceilings, one room holding various equipment from the gin, the other half-full of unshucked corn. Because the ears of corn stacked higher on one side of the crib than the other, we could "mountain climb" up the pile of corn until our weight made the corn avalanche down and we rode it. Sometimes we ended up buried underneath the corn pile, as if we'd be buried and never found, a part of the game we loved best. It was during one of these adventures that I fell into my first regrettable trouble at Union High, troubling because it revealed in me a budding conscience.

Truth is, my "conscience" had pretty much remained underground during eight years and a few months of stubborn innocence, refusing to enter debates between "right" and "wrong." Sure, I knew some things, like the German bombers which troubled my dreams, and some people, like Billy Joe, scared the heck out of me. I also understood that I enjoyed doing some things, like reading comic books, and hated doing other things, like chopping cotton. Certainly, my mother's carrying on about Daddy dying and us being the poorest people in the whole world made me uneasy, but that was my mother's load to carry, not mine. I was merely the kid on a slightly cloudy day, looking in the window at a chilly melodrama.

To put myself in another person's place and sympathize with them, good or bad, like if they won a million dollars on a punch board or if they fell down a well with a load of bricks, had not yet happened in my emotional makeup. It's a wonderment, then, that it only took a fifty-cents-worth lesson to startle the infernal machinery of my "conscience" into working.

One late afternoon found Momma and me in our room at the house after coming in from the cotton patch. I'd sailed my straw hat onto a chair and was shucking off my clod hoppers, now intending to enjoy some barefoot time, shake off the field. Momma always wore a slit bonnet and a denim jumper in the field, and she still had on her sweat-stained jumper when she mentioned I'd better go up to the store, which was alright by me. Maybe there'd be a few cents for me to spend on candy balls or Tootsie Rolls.

"It's our night to get fixings for supper," she said. "Aunt Sis said she'd make us up some milk gravy and biscuits, except we don't have no condensed milk." She went to the dresser and opened a drawer and took out her black purse. "I want you to go get two big cans of Carnation milk. Everybody's hungry as I am, they don't want to wait long for hot biscuits." She took out the coin purse Daddy used to carry around and unsnapped it.

"Momma, can I have a nickel for jaw-breakers? I promise I won't suck on them till after supper."

"No, Baby, they ain't money for extra. You get the condensed milk, that's all."

She put a fifty-cent piece in my hand and closed my fingers over it and snapped the coin purse closed.

"That fifty cents is the only money we got until Mr. Keitt pays everybody on Saturday. You get change, we can help Wylie and them out with supper on Friday." She tapped my closed hand with a finger as if to change the fifty-cent piece into a hundred dollars by magic. "That's how much you get for chopping Johnson grass tomorrow." She smiled and gave me a little push. "Now don't let no lice grow on you."

I collected Melvin Junior, whose red hair was still damp from wearing his waxed, red hat all day in the field, and Frankie, who'd been laying around the house, bare-footed and wearing overalls, too little to chop cotton, and we headed up the road toward the store. The dirt road felt good under my own bare feet.

"Aunt Bill give you a dollar?" Melvin Junior was hoping for penny candy.

"Nope. Give me this fifty-cent piece," I said, showing it to him and Frankie. Since I usually only handled a nickel or a dime, seldom a quarter, never fifty cents, I liked the feel of the coin's weight in my hand. It felt and looked like silver, and there was a woman in a long, flowing dress striding across one side of the coin. I looked at the date in tiny numbers: 1939. Everything about the coin was rich, like as if you had a pocketful you'd be rich too.

"Momma said only buy condensed milk. It's all our money till Saturday."

"Uncle Bud said it's Sat-ta-day, 'cause it's payday," said Frankie. I wasn't sure what he meant, but that was alright. He didn't have anybody to play with all day but girls.

Two or three Model-As were parked near the store when we got there. Several men in overalls were standing in a group on the porch, talking about the weather. The three of us went to the end of the porch that looked off toward the storage shed.

"Ain't nobody at the shed," said Melvin Junior. "Let's go jump on that damn corn."

"Can't," I reminded him. "Momma said get back home to hot biscuits."

"Look yonder at the sun," he said, pointing toward the horizon where pink clouds let the sun's rays struggle through. "It's a hour before dark. Supper ain't nearly ready. We got time to play in the crib a minute or two, and Frankie wants to jump on the damn corn. He said so."

I looked at Frankie. "Let's jump on the damn corn," he said.

Maybe we could play in the crib for a few minutes. Anyway, it was more fun than I'd had all day in the cotton patch.

As we approached the door of the corn crib, I put my fifty-cent coin in a front pocket of my overalls. I already had a Coca Cola bottle cap and two marbles and a piece of quartz I'd found in the field in there. The coin fitted right in.

Sure enough, we had the crib to ourselves. We got right into the corn, and Frankie threw ears of corn around like he was a soldier grenade thrower, but he mainly banged Melvin Junior and me upside the head. Every time we'd climb up the mountain of corn it would avalanche down with us riding it, and we'd be mostly buried by it. Soon there was a thick cloud of shuck dust in the crib.

"Let's play like the corn is a tank of water, and dive in head fomus," called Melvin Junior. We dived and swam around until we had corn shuck down our collars and chaff in our hair. Frankie cut a finger on a dry corn shuck and started to bawl.

"We better get back to the store," I said. I wondered how much time we'd played in the corn. Not long I hoped, so we wouldn't have to tell where we'd been.

We ran back to the store, Frankie crying over his cut finger.

The men were gone when we stepped up on the porch, so we could go right in the store and get the condensed milk. I put my hand in the pocket of my overalls, feeling for my fifty-cent piece, and all I brought out was a piece of quartz. I checked my other pocket and found nothing. Back in the other pocket, my hand dug deep and came out empty, not even a Coca Cola bottle cap, and--worst of all--no silver coin. I had lost the fifty-cent piece in the corn crib!

"We got to go back and look for my fifty cents," I yelled, and started running back to the storage crib. I was dumb with fear. How could I have lost Momma's money?

Back inside the crib the three of us stirred the corn around, shoveled it back and forth with our hands, kicked it with our feet, and tried to dig to the floor in case the coin had settled all the way down. But there was so much corn, plenty for making up rough games, but more than we could manage in a search for a single fifty-cent piece. We tried to stack the ears of corn into piles, but they only fell down, scattering all over. Soon we got into each other's way with violent digging and threshing around, always making our stacks of corn avalanche downward around our ankles. Our search was fueled by fear and desperation, but at last we knew it was hopeless. The coin was lost. As I closed the door to the corn crib, I stood and looked at all that damn corn, and willed the fifty-cent piece to fall out somewhere, but magic failed me and it didn't.

How was I going to explain to Momma that our last fifty cents was gone, and we had no condensed milk for hot biscuits? As the three of us walked along the road, my brain seemed to be on fire with thinking about what I could say when we got home.

"Say we got robbed by some old sot drunk with a gun," suggested Melvin Junior.

"If Leon got run over by a car, he wouldn't have to tell Aunt Bill," said Frankie, who was still nursing a finger that bled once in a while, though his bawling was mostly being a baby.

Both my overall pockets were turned inside out. It was unbelievable the coin was not in there somewhere. I'd searched both my back pockets and the bib pocket in case it had moved around without me knowing it. Not even a Coca Cola bottle cap showed up.

I tried to come up with some believable excuse for having played in the corn instead of buying the condensed milk and going right back to the house. That first mistake, I knew, led to the lost money, an even worse bad thing I'd done. The more I realized I'd never get away with any stories or lies, the more I figured I'd have to tell the truth. And the thought of telling Momma the truth filled me with outrageous fright. Maybe Frankie was right, it would be better for me if I got run over by a car. I wouldn't care if I died.

When we got to our front yard, Uncle Bud and my cousin Katie were sitting on the porch steps. Katie liked to hear Uncle Bud's stories about the old days.

"Well, you'all look at what the cat drug in," said Uncle Bud, greeting us.

"Leon lost all the money and we can't have no supper," said Frankie, busting a gut to be first with bad news.

"Gambling is a sin worse than stealing chickens," said Uncle Bud, laughing at his joke.

"I ain't been gambling," I said. "It fell out of my pocket in the corn crib."

Momma had come to the door, probably wondering what happened to us, ready to get the biscuits and gravy before sundown. She came out on the porch, a kitchen apron on now.

"You mean to tell me you'all lost that fifty cents and don't have no Carnation milk?"

I began to cry right in front of everybody. I couldn't help myself. I'd get a whipping to sting my legs, bad enough, but my sense of having done a direful thing stung me in a different place. I was conscious of how things could have been different: hot biscuits and milk gravy on the table, us all drinking iced tea, Uncle Bud making some jokes, Uncle Wylie talking about going on a squirrel hunt, Momma and Aunt Sis spooning out some red beans on our plates, the little kids eating and staring at the grownups, being quiet. Now it wouldn't be the same because of my bad behavior.

And it wasn't the same. We had our gravy, but it was made with water instead of milk. If you've ever seen water gravy, you know it looks like paste used for hanging wall paper, all gray and sticky. So we slopped the gravy on pieces of day-old Rainbow light-bread, no way as good as hot biscuits. That meant nobody was as jolly as new-made biscuits and milk gravy will never fail to make you. My own supper kind of stuck in my throat that night.

Fortunately for me, I guess, my mother was open to signs of penance. She didn't switch me for my misbehavior, said she thought I'd "suffered enough already," which--she said--was my conscience bothering me. Later that evening in our room she gave me a talking-to, which in some ways was more painful than a spanking. To give me a lesson, she laid out a grocery ad from a newspaper to show me what our fifty cents would've bought if we'd had it. There was my damnation set out in fuzzy newsprint: a dozen winesap apples for a nickel; box of corn flakes for a dime; can of Campbell's tomato soup for seven cents; ten pounds of potatoes for seventeen cents; even a broom for a penny.

"Looky here," said Momma, pointing to the drawing of a smiling man dressed in a fine shirt he was proud of. "We could of bought you a nice blue chambry work shirt for thirty-three cents."

Of course, I couldn't bring myself to be impressed by anything having to do with work, even a blue chambry shirt, but I saw how I'd thrown away all them apples and Post Toasties and a new broom in the corn. Momma preached to me all over again that I'd lost our last fifty cents until we'd get paid on Saturday, and then our money was pay for whatever cotton chopping we did all week. Because I was worth only half as much as a grown-up field hand, I made fifty cents a day. Because I'd lost my fifty cents, I had chopped cotton all one afternoon in the hot sun for nothing. Boy, I felt most awful I'd ever felt.

As often could happen, a talking-to led to carrying on by Momma.

"Baby, you didn't mind me and look what happened," she began. "Some people say when a boy don't have no daddy, it's awful hard for his momma to keep an eye on all the mess he can get into. I know you need a daddy, but it scares me to think about marrying some old man who'd be mean to you. That's why your momma is trying to raise you up all by herself, save you from a daddy you'd find hateful." She was looking at me through those magnifying glasses, so I had to be really still and listen to her talking. And all the time I kept seeing a picture in my mind of a big ape-like giant coming after me with a razor strop.

"I sure don't want no daddy," I confessed. "I know they'd all be mean and scare us to pieces." Still, I wasn't sure what a daddy had to do with anything. I felt really bad about losing our money in the corn crib, especially because it meant Momma and everybody had to eat old water gravy on light-bread for supper. "But I wish I had the fifty cents back so I could give it to you and Aunt Sis for condensed milk. Seems like everybody lost something when I lost the fifty cents in the damn corn."

I guess my mother and I both realized at the same time what I'd blurted out.

"Lord have mercy, Leon, you starting to talk like Papa."

I could see that Momma wondered how on earth she was going to raise a boy like me, and all I wanted was to let her know I was sorry about the corn crib. It was looking to me like life at Union High was going to be one tough row to hoe unless this conscience thing let up on me.

Chapter 10

A COLORED BOY AT THE COTTON WAGON

One Sunday afternoon late in August, 1940, I sat on the front porch with my Uncle Bud, watching him fix his ducking sack for picking cotton, a job we'd all start the next day. The sack was at least ten feet long, three or four feet longer than cotton sacks pulled by most people, for Uncle Bud picked more cotton than most people. He'd already sewed on the shoulder strap over the open mouth of the sack, the strap he'd pull the sack with as he straddled the rows, picking the cotton from the opened bolls. Now he was twisting a piece of baling wire around one corner of the bottom of the sack, inside of which he'd stuck a green cotton boll to anchor the wire, so he could hang a full sack of cotton on the scales to weigh it. Sometimes he'd weigh up seventy or eighty pounds of cotton in the sack. The new ducking, made of cotton fabric, gave off a pleasant waxy smell, not unlike that of a canvas sideshow tent if you used your imagination.

"Uncle Bud," I asked, "why is it that cotton picking and school always start at the same time?"

"Well, don't you see," he said, "it's a ways of keeping kids that ask questions from going to the state penitentiary at Huntsville." He gave the baling wire a final twist.

I knew he was joking, as he often did. I'd become used to that. It was one of the reasons I'd come to think of him as "favorite uncle," though Uncle Wylie was also a favorite. But we were going to take our sacks to the fields in the morning and begin picking Mr. Joe Keitt's cotton, a job that would last into December, then in two weeks I'd have to start the second grade in another new school for me, now at Union High. Momma had already explained to me in detail that Melvin Junior and me'd go to school in the mornings, then hike ourselves to the cotton patch right after school let out. Since we lived so close to school, me and him would come right on to the house, change our clothes, eat some peanut butter and crackers, and get to the field. It'd be no fooling around. We'd get to pick cotton for about four hours every day. She'd already made my cotton sack, a short one, long as I was tall, just rake the ground when I stood up. It lay on the porch close enough to me that I could smell its newness.

"I feel like I might not like this old school in Union High," I said.

Uncle Bud stood up and shook out the cotton sack to its full length and tugged at the strap, testing his needle and thread work. He was a few years younger than my mother, but didn't look it because his hair was thinning, and he always wore farmer's work shoes and blue overalls. And yet there was that joking, child-like quality about

Uncle Bud that made him less sober than most grown-ups, so you could listen to him without feeling he'd put you in your place.

"You can feel like it if you want to," he said. "Nobody ain't goin' to sic a dog on you. But you might want to wait and find out how you feel about picking cotton tomorrow before you get married to a cotton sack."

When I debuted the next morning as a cotton picker on Mr. Joe Keitt's place at the age of eight years and three months, I had only a half-complete understanding of the nature of the job. Back on Mr. David's place I had seen my sister Lucy and my mother and other grown-ups sling bulging tamped-down sacks of cotton over their shoulders and carry them over the rows to the wagon to weigh up on the scales. It made you think of something way out of history when you saw those cotton pickers slow-walk between the rows, cotton sacks stretched and bulging like huge larva of beasts they'd killed in the forest. The people looked puny, loaded down, but there was an air of proudness about them. They seemed to be saying, "I can't pick a bale of cotton! Well, don't you bet on it!" Anybody who could do that looked awful grown-up to me.

But my own history with cotton at that time issued from the few bolls I'd cleaned out and put into my mother's sack as I wandered along beside her. One serious thing I'd not learned, then, was that picking cotton was a scramble. Since a field hand in the cotton patch was paid about a dollar a hundred pounds weighed up, that meant the more you picked the more you earned. Pick less and you'd be paid less. So picking cotton was a hurried struggle against time to get as much cotton out of the bolls and into the sack as you could. Hands and eyes working together against the sun's passage concentrated the worker's mind on his or her row of cotton stalks in the fixed attitude of a cat sneaking up on a goose. Let the mind wander into thoughts about a comic book or fried chicken, and the game was lost. And if your mother noticed you dragging an empty sack, you'd feel like the goose had got the cat.

Another thing I learned immediately, according to grown-ups who ran the show, was you couldn't get to the cotton patch too early or stay too late. I ran into that side of the job on my first day in the field. Mr. Waller had us all in the cotton patch the next morning before sun-up. Since it was too dry for it to be any dew on the cotton plants, all we had to do was wait for the sun to catch up with us. Melvin Junior had picked cotton before and wasn't excited about another season of it, so he pitched his cotton sack on the ground, lay down on it, and pretended to sleep. I, on the other hand, was wide awake from excitement about finally getting to pick cotton with my own sack. To me that meant I was grown-up. Actually, without an inkling, I was beginning a chapter in the history of growing up which would last through the next decade.

Momma had cut and sewed me a new book satchel out of ducking at the same time she made my cotton sack. Someplace along the line of our moves since I'd toted my first book satchel off to the first grade, we had lost it, even though it had my name printed on it with indelible ink. But I guess my mother hadn't lost her faith that I'd get back into school and finish the second grade before I grew up. The new satchel was a sign of her faith. Even though she had sewed a button from a work jumper on it to hold down a flap over the top, I thought it looked fine. After picking cotton in my other sack for two weeks, I was ready to give school a chance.

Taking me out of the field and sending me to school for much of the day was obviously a tough decision for my mother. As I got some experience with picking cotton, found my hands toughened up, learned how to ease my back by crawling along the row on my knees, I began to get more cotton in my little sack, and weighed up maybe eighty pounds a day. Because I was now making between eighty cents and a dollar a day, I was helping my mother with grocery money. To send me out of the field a half day meant a smaller contribution by me. Mr. Waller pointed this out to Momma at the supper table the night before school started the next day.

"You takin' that young'un out of the field just when he gets to be worth his salt." He then scowled across the table at me as if I was a farm tool that broke down. "Don't make a damn bit of sense. You ain't got no money to speak of the way it is."

None of us kids ever said much at the supper table, just listened to the grown-ups talk about work. I was surprised when Frankie spoke up.

"If Leon hadn't lost Aunt Bill's fifty cents, she'd have some money," he piped up.

"Hush up, Frankie," said Aunt Ett. "Eat your supper."

Aunt Sis had soaked a big pot of butter beans all day and fixed them for supper. I really loved butter beans and corn bread, but I didn't care much for collard greens. I just kept on mashing up my corn bread in my butter beans, but I was kind of holding my breath, because I was afraid Mr. Waller would change Momma's mind about me going to school. I felt better when she spoke up.

"I ain't taking Leon out of school long as I've got breath. He's already lost too much time and got behind as it is," Momma said.

"You always took us kids out of school, Papa. You made me and Ett and Bud chop and pick cotton while other kids went on to school. And you look at us today. We ain't got nothing, and you ain't neither."

"Bill's right about that, Papa. You can't deny it," Aunt Sis put in. "We're sending our kids to school to get an education. Maybe they can do something besides chop and pick cotton."

"I wish I could pick cotton," said Frankie.

"Be quiet, Frankie,"said Aunt Ett. "Eat them beans on your plate."

Uncle Bud rattled the ice around in his sweet tea glass, and allowed as how if you knew how to spell Mississippi you didn't need to go to school and could stay home like rich people.

"Leon," he looked at me and grinned, "you know how to spell Mississippi?"

"No," I said, "I ain't been to school enough."

Then he asked Katie Ruth, and she spelled it "M-i-s-s-i-s-s-i-p-p-i." Katie looked pretty sure of her spelling, because she was good in school.

"Nope," said Uncle Bud. "You spell it 'Mi-crooked letter, crooked letter, i-crooked letter, crooked letter, i-hump back, hump back, i.'" He looked at us as though he'd mystified us, laughed and said, "I guess I get to stay home like a rich man."

The next morning four of us kids left Mr. Waller, already wearing a straw hat, cussing on the front porch about wasting good field hands "to dadgum go to school." Uncle Wylie was leaning on a porch post smoking a cigarette, and he just told us to go on to school. Melvin Junior, sporting a fresh haircut Uncle Bud had given him, was headed for the third grade, which he'd passed into by the skin of his teeth, and Katie Ruth, who liked to study and got all good grades, was going into the fourth grade, but she had to look after Frankie, just starting first grade. I, of course, had nothing to show for last year except a report card sopped in red ink, so was retreating into second grade in a school I knew nothing about or what to expect, except Melvin Junior said, "Look out," everybody picked on you, get ready.

The Union High grammar school was a white box-like building of two stories, supporting an iron fire escape on the side next to the road. A bunch of windows looked out past the fire escape at the road. The school's spacious playground spread out along the road leading to the gin and store, and at recess you'd see teams pulling cotton wagons to the gin, where mules and wagons and farmers waited turns to pull through the sheds and have the cotton suctioned up into the lofts where the fibers and seeds were separated. To see mules dozing in their harness and farmers standing around the wagons jawing about their crops invited you to feel lazy and peaceful in the morning heat. However, clues to a more rowdy pack of country boys on the Union High schoolyard soon exposed themselves to me, the first person to be in favor of peace, the last to find it.

Because news about the war in Europe filled all the magazines and newspapers, even more so on the radio for people who had them, it had become common for boys to play "soldier." Even my comic books, when I could get a new one, warned about saboteurs coming ashore in rubber rafts. In a copy of a *Wings* comic book I'd found, there were dogfights in the sky and aviators parachuting out of burning Spitfires, and it also had pictures of the bombers I dreamed about. So it wasn't long after I started at Union High that playing "soldier" led to a game at recess in which boys hid in the bar ditch of the nearby road and threw dirt-clod "bombs" at passing cars, then ran like rabbits when the cars slowed. One day a man whose car had been "bombed" to a standstill jumped out and chased the "soldiers." Two were caught and taken to a teacher, who paddled them in his office. The man from the car watched, said, "It's about time," whatever that meant.

Several encounters I had with these boys persuaded me to spend most of my recess time inside the school house. At first they picked on me because my ears stuck out. "Elephant ears! Elephant ears!" After that joke grew old, they graduated to the classic school-ground trickery, shoving me over a boy who'd sneaked up and kneeled behind me. One thing led to another until the tough boys associated me with Melvin Junior, known as "Red," who had fights that drew crowds of kids and teachers to break things up, me stuck on the sidelines like the concealed rabbit in the Sunday-paper picture puzzle.

Inside the school room I was doing pretty well in the second grade. I read better than most of the other second graders, for I'd read everything I got my hands on since I'd left Hubbard Elementary. I ate and breathed comic books, and when my sister Lucy came in a Model A to visit us, she'd bring me saved-up stacks of *Life* and *Saturday Evening Post* magazines to feed my appetite for reading. Our arithmetic lessons were easy for me, and I enjoyed writing with our new pencils, sometimes tracing airplanes from magazines. Lucky for me, I had a teacher who treated me kindly, even when I stayed inside at recess. She probably also rescued small, lost animals.

Walking home after school was the most dangerous part of the day. First thing on the way home we had to get out of the schoolyard, crowded as a Greyhound depot. There was no school bus, a few kids might ride on an empty cotton wagon passing along the road, but most kids walked home as we did. Picking on "Red" before we got off the school ground was as normal as recess. Name-calling came first, then shoving and pushing, which led to wrestling on the ground, which ended in a dogfight with everybody jumping on the wrestler who seemed to be on top.

One afternoon me and Melvin Junior had reached the dusty, cleared-off area called "the softball diamond," lying near the corner closest to the store and gin. We had to get home and change into our work clothes and get off to the field, pick as much cotton as we could before sundown. I was in a special hurry because I'd shamed Momma into buying me a pair of cowboy shoes, and I needed to make up for some of the cost of the shoes. My real lesson from this affair was I'd learned the kinship between the old devil conscience and shame. The Sears Roebuck picture of the shoes--not full high-topped boots, but lace-up, ankle-high shoes with cowboy heels and pointed toes--had so kindled my "need" for them that I'd cried and begged and, finally, stormed at my mother: "If Daddy was alive, he'd buy me them cowboy shoes!" This shameless outburst so affected my mother with guilt that she took the Bull Durham bag of dimes and ordered the shoes for me. Daddy's dimes were gone. Today, I was wearing my shameless cowboy shoes.

Four or five sixth-grade girls, toting books and lunch pails, stood at the corner talking and laughing. Two of them were pretty. The others were ugly. As we were passing them, a couple of the girls began to shout in our direction.

"Booger Red! Booger Red! Ugliest man living or dead!"

Instead of going on, we stopped.

"You'all's so ugly I'd hate to see your underpants," Melvin Junior shouted back.

"Booger Red, ought to be dead," called one girl, and threw an apple at Melvin Junior, which he caught and flung back and struck her upside the head.

Now all the girls charged us over the few yards of separation and began swinging books and lunch pails. Even the two pretty girls were powerful and mean, hitting at both of us. Melvin Junior tripped one girl and grabbed a lunch pail from another one, but two girls began grabbing and pulling his hair. I struck one of the girls on the arm with my book satchel, which made two girls turn on me with their lunch pails and bang my hand when I protected my head. Two of the girls managed to trip Melvin Junior to the ground and began hitting him with books and pails. The scuffle made a little cloud of dust. I pulled loose from the two girls who struck me, slapped one across the nose, and ran for the road. I looked back to see Melvin Junior kicking with his feet at several girls, one of them flailing him with a ruler. Batman was down, Robin took to his heels.

Uncle Bud happened to be at the house when I arrived, out of breath and panting. And from that day on his favorite story he'd tell, laughing so hard tears rolled down his cheeks, was about hearing me coming down the road fast as I could.

"You could hear Leon's cowboy boots pounding on the road a half mile off!"

It wasn't long after I started at Union High that the school began serving hot food for all the kids who couldn't bring nutritious lunches. This was good news for me, as well as for my cousins, because we were too poor to bring more than peanut butter and jelly. And we didn't get much nutrition at home beyond red beans, cornbread, condensed-milk gravy, and collard greens. Before going to school it was usually coffee and biscuits for breakfast. Momma sometimes wept, she said, when she saw the good breakfasts of eggs and bacon the people ate where she cleaned house in the mornings, as she knew Melvin Junior and me'd gone off to school hungry. For the school lunches we ate hot dogs or hamburgers or soups and fried potatoes, then had desserts of cake or pudding. The only bad thing about the school lunch was the teachers sat with us at little tables, and we learned table manners like napkins and soup spoons. I thought the manners took some fun out of eating.

Since the teachers didn't include girls as a subject in class, that subject for me was left up to Melvin Junior, two years older and savvy.

"Leon," he set the subject in motion one day coming home from school, "I bet you ain't never even kissed a single girl."

"Why'd I want to do that?"

"Any boy don't kiss a girl is a sissy," Melvin Junior explained.

The thought of kissing a girl had never crossed my mind. I didn't even like girls I knew. Somehow liking girls and kissing girls were linked together in my mind. I knew that Daisy Mae was always chasing Li'l Abner all over Dogpatch in my *Tip Top* comic book, but Li'l Abner was as disgusted with her as I was. Besides, since he never kissed Daisy Mae, I didn't have any idea how the thing was done.

"I bet I'd like to know how many girls you've kissed," I said, stopping him in his tracks.

"Shoot, about a hunderd last time I counted," he said.

Well, that did seem to put Melvin Junior well ahead of me who'd never kissed any girl. He finally said, "If you're going to run with us big boys you can't be no sissy." He stopped and pointed to a house down a ways from ours. "They's a girl in that house." The way he said it seemed to mean I was to go to that house, walk up in the yard, check for no dog, step right up on the porch, knock on the door, and kiss a girl when she showed up. Then I wouldn't be no sissy.

Frankie was in the yard digging a hole with a shovel when we got there. He dug holes in the yard every day after school. He said it would rain and they'd fill up with crawfish.

"Melvin Junior says you're a sissy if you ain't kissed no girl," I told him.

"I'll tell Aunt Sis if he says I'm a sissy," he said, and dug some more dirt.

As usual we changed into work clothes and went to the field with our cotton sacks. But it makes no sense to pick cotton and think about kissing girls at the same time. I'd find myself just standing still holding a cotton boll in my hand, a behavior my mother called "Letting dead lice fall off you," which made her yell at me to pick up my row. I knew I'd have to put off the business with girls until later or I'd find myself in trouble.

My conscience came back into my life a few days later like it had not given up on me, but it had nothing to do with girls. Me and Melvin Junior had picked our first sackfuls of cotton after school, which found us at the wagon to weigh up our sacks at the same time.

A woman I didn't know was keeping weights for us, adding them up on a cardboard. So while me and him drank water from our family's water jug, kept cool underneath the wagon in the shade, she penciled our balances of pounds of cotton in a big ledger book. We climbed up into the wagon and emptied our cotton on the big pile. When I jumped down to the ground, I landed beside a kid about my size, a colored boy who'd dragged a sack of cotton up to the scales. He was wearing a straw hat a bit too big and blue overalls with knee patches, and he looked as tired as I felt. He was bare- footed, standing there in the sand.

"Hey," I said, but he didn't say anything. I picked up my empty sack and draped it over my shoulder.

"We only got here after school," I said, "and I already weighed up twenty pounds. Looks like you got about that, too." He didn't say anything, so I asked, "You just back from school?"

"No, ma'm," he said, and stood there looking at his sack of cotton. He hardly moved.

"What grade you in? I'm back in second, but it's easy," I said as I waited for Melvin Junior to get off the wagon

The boy looked at his sack of cotton as though it would answer for him.

"Ain't no grade," he finally said.

Melvin Junior threw his cotton sack to the ground and climbed off the wagon. He picked up his sack and whacked me with its strap.

"Let's go," he said. "He don't go to no school. He's a little nigger boy."

The boy didn't look at us as we walked off with our empty sacks.

"All them colored people live back of the tank in their own place," Melvin Junior told me when we started picking again. "Mr. Keitt lets them stay there."

"Don't that kid ever play with nobody?" I was studying on it as I began to pick my row.

Maybe because I'd been laid-off from going to school when Momma took me to stay in Corsicana, maybe because I'd felt left behind by everybody after failing second grade, I couldn't stop wondering why the boy at the wagon didn't go to school because he was a nigger. It seemed to me like everybody went to school and that was that. I'd been sure I wasn't head over heels crazy about going to school in Hubbard, but when I couldn't go I'd found all kinds of reasons I wanted to go. Maybe that boy was like me at first, didn't want to go to school, maybe felt good about it. Of course, I'd never talked to a colored boy before. At Mr. David's it was the families who lived there doing all the cotton chopping and cotton picking. And yet I knew there were colored people in town, buying groceries, talking with each other on sidewalks. You'd see little colored kids running on the streets, sometimes hanging on their mother's hand. From talk by grownups I knew that some people called them "niggers" and some people called them "colored folks." But they were just there, as I was just there, and it wasn't something I'd thought about. At least not until I almost jumped off the wagon on this kid.

"Leon! You boys in the cotton sacks, pick up them rows." It was Momma who'd noticed me standing up. She yelled from farther up the field, where she was pulling a nearly-full sack of cotton, ready to weigh up. "The dead lice won't fall off you'all!"

153

The next afternoon me and Melvin Junior finished picking our hundred pounds a while before quitting time, and Momma had said we could quit after we got our hundred pounds. We emptied our cotton in the wagon and threw the empty sacks down beside the water jug and we took off running. We had some free time to look for adventure.

Today Melvin Junior said why didn't we go over behind the tank and look at where the little nigger kids played. When we got over there, it looked like everybody was off in the cotton patch, no little kids around the yards. There were three cabins where people lived, all of them smaller than our house. Chimneys stood at the end of each cabin, and there was one window and one door on the side near the front yard. The yard in front of one cabin was hard dirt swept clean, probably with a straw broom the way Momma swept our front yard. It didn't have any flowers, but there was a wash pot like the one Aunt Anna had at her wood pile. Me and Melvin Junior walked across the yard, stopped to look at a hungry-appearing kitten playing in a cardboard box, and went to a narrow set of board steps leading up to an open front door, not even a screen.

"Might's well go inside and look," said Melvin Junior. "Nobody ain't home."

There were two rooms inside, a kitchen and a bedroom. A kerosene cookstove with blackened burners stood in a corner, opposite from a square wood table on which were laid out several crockery plates and loose spoons and forks. Three or four chairs with unraveling cane bottoms sat around the table. Somebody had cut out and pasted newspaper and magazine pictures on the walls of the kitchen. One picture showed President Roosevelt, another picture showed a soldier smoking a Lucky Strike. I kind of liked that, wished we had some on our walls.

Melvin Junior had gone into the bedroom, and I followed. A big iron bedstead took up half the room, and a frayed quilt made a bed cover. The cabin's one window looked out through the front wall beyond the bed, leaving the room semi-dark. A painted picture of Jesus hung above the iron headboard of the bed. Across the room from the bed stood a chest of drawers. Laid across the top of the chest were little jars and bottles and a comb and mirror. Some of the drawers in the chest had no drawer pulls.

I watched as Melvin Junior jimmied one of the drawers out. I was curious about what we'd find in the drawer and went to look. I was poking my hand into the drawer when I heard a voice from the kitchen door.

"What you boys doin' in here?"

My heart went into my throat as I looked and saw a large colored woman blocking the door. By the way she was dressed in a faded blue shirt and a long skirt and carried a straw hat in one hand I guessed she'd just come in from the field where we'd all been picking cotton. She walked into the room and stood near the dresser and me and Melvin Junior. She pushed the drawers closed.

"I know where you boys is, 'cause I seen you'all in the patch with Mr. Waller them." She laid her hat on the bed and placed a hand on the bedstead as though she were very tired and needed support. "I'm sorry to find you white boys here messin' in the dresser."

Cold fear had paralyzed me where I stood. I couldn't speak, even if I'd had any words to explain what we were doing in the dresser. Melvin Junior was likewise infected with paralysis.

155

"I 'spect you'all's mamma don't know you's here." She was looking right at me as if I'd begun to glow in the dark. "We ain't got no door to lock up noways, so I guess white boys don't think it's no mor'n a shack on the place. You'all's home don't look this a way." She sat down on the edge of the bed, whether because she was tired out or to get on our level I couldn't have said. She could look right into my wide eyes that saw nothing now save for a wearied dark face and her own accusing gaze. "We stays in Mr. Keitt's house and works his cotton same's you'all do, but you'all's white folks. Still, that don't give white boys leave to come in nowhere we stay and meddle in our truck. We'se niggers, but we got feelin's and family like rest of you'all people." The woman facing me rose slowly to her feet and walked toward the kitchen door. "You'all go home, now. I got to make my chilren supper."

Me and Melvin Junior ran home without stopping. Over the next few days we hardly talked about what had happened. I think we were waiting for the colored woman to tell on us to Momma or to Mr. Waller, hoping that what was not talked about would not come to pass. But the woman never told and Momma didn't find out, even with eyes in the back of her head.

In the silence that followed, however, my "conscience," which had more or less laid low since the loss of Momma's fifty-cent piece, awakened with the righteous indignation of a street preacher I'd witnessed once as a little kid while toting a new *Tip Top* comic book. In my mind, sleeping or waking, I kept meeting over and over the woman who'd found us pilfering things in her house. I'd see her leaning wearily against the iron bedstead, while hearing her words: "We got feelin's and family like the rest of you'all people."

Something, maybe that troublesome, bothering "conscience," kept telling me that she was right, and that what me and Melvin Junior had done was about the worst thing I'd ever done. I figured even you could lose fifty cents and maybe find another one just lying in the road one day, but there was some unnameable thing wrong with "nigger," and I'd have to make that out as I went along.

Melvin Junior didn't give up on adventures for me and Frankie, though. He soon had us fishing for chickens out our back bedroom window, which had no screen on it. We'd made a fishing pole from a broom handle, on which we nailed one of Aunt Sis' empty thread-spools, then wound up some string with a fish hook on the end. A bunch of old hens scratched and pecked around on the ground beyond the window, so it was natural to put corn on the hook and cast it outside among the hens. Usually they ignored the "bait," but one day we caught a Rhode Island Red that raised a terrible racket when we tried to reel her into the bedroom. Katie Ruth told Aunt Ett what we'd done, and she came storming like an old mad hen herself into the bedroom, to find the chicken reel in Frankie's hands, plus a pillow we'd poked down his overalls.

"Melvin Junior and Leon beat me up and made me fish for chickens," he said. Aunt Ett gave him two spankings, one for the chicken, one for telling lies.

My own spanking came about as a result of trying to kiss a girl. Melvin Junior insisted if I'd give a piece of candy to that girl in the next house, she'd let me kiss her, then I'd never in my life have to worry about being a sissy. Since each of us had a penny, we went to the store and bought a two-cent "candy" cigar, which turned out to be a "rubber" cigar. It looked life-like, firm and about the color and shape of a cigar, and was wrapped in cellophane. It was hard to tell from a real Cuban, we told ourselves. Since nobody was at our house after school, we watched for the neighbor girl, who walked along Main Street Union High going home.

"Hey, you want a piece of candy?" I was standing near the road with the rubber cigar.

She was undeniably a pretty girl, a fourth-grader, and she wore nice dresses and fixed her hair with clips. She came into the yard swinging a leather book satchel.

"What kind of candy?"

I showed her the cigar, still in its cellophane wrapper. It had a grownup look to it.

"It's a candy cigar, but it looks real and cost two cents," I explained.

She took the wrapping off, and mashed the cigar with her fingers.

"It's rubber. It's not candy," she said. She put down her book satchel, looking interested anyway, even if it was rubber. "You can chew on it just the way people do real cigars."

She put the cigar in her mouth and chewed one end of it. It made squishy noises. She began to make funny faces, then took out the cigar which had begun to take on a soggy look.

I wasn't sure how I was supposed to go about the kiss, because she didn't seem to be carried away with the "candy."

"I'll give you the cigar to keep if you give me a kiss," I blurted out.

She threw the cigar on the ground and stepped on it and picked up her satchel.

"I ain't never kissed no boy, and I ain't never going to," she said, "and when I do it won't be you." She stalked back to Main Street Union High. I thought she looked mad, but Melvin Junior said it was the way girls acted. Since we had paid two cents for the cigar, we decided to make use of it, and we both chewed on it where the girl had messed it up. It was wet and soggy and after a while we both felt sick, and still had to change our clothes and go to the cotton patch.

When we got to the field with our cotton sacks, Momma met me with a cotton stalk in her hand. She was pretty mad.

"I ain't having you stopping no girls on the way home. It don't look good," she informed me, then switched me with the stalk. I didn't even ask how she already knew I'd done it. Mothers had eyes in the back of their heads, and you couldn't do anything without them knowing it.

By Christmas time in 1940, after the cotton crop was laid by, we found out big changes were on the way. It looked like 1941 was going to be a year with big things happening. We first learned we'd be moving early next year to a place called Bowmandale, where-ever in the world that might be. Mr. Joe Keitt had some cotton there he'd want chopped at the end of Spring, and me and Melvin Junior would start a new school. Uncle Wylie, Aunt Sis, Katie Ruth, Frankie, and "that mess of kids" wouldn't be going with us. Just me and Momma, and Mr. Waller, Uncle Bud, and Melvin Junior.

That Christmas I got a silver-barrel cowboy pistol, with a long-horn steer on the handle grip. It was brought by Santa Claus, who we tried to sneak up on in a dark room but couldn't. Best gift of all, though: I found out I was to be promoted to the third grade at Christmas. My teacher said I had beautiful handwriting!

Chapter 11

SAWIN' OFF A LEG

Calina, Texas, a community we'd just moved to, only me and Momma and Mr. Waller, and Uncle Bud and Melvin Junior, was at peace on my ninth birthday, the third of June, 1941. The rest of the world was at war. It showed in *Life* magazine. They'd had a artist draw a map of every place in Europe, and the artist painted a blazing fire everywhere Hitler put his foot down. You couldn't count on the fingers of one hand the countries didn't have German soldiers. It was just pitiful. I told Momma about it. She said, "I told everybody it'd be a mess if that Hitler got elected."

I didn't know how Momma knew that, because we didn't have a radio in our house. But it seemed like everybody you talked to in Hill County, they'd say the same thing. All I had working for me was the pictures in *Life* magazine.

On my ninth birthday Momma explained to me how we were between cotton picking and cotton chopping, so we'd had no work to get paid for, and she couldn't buy me a present, but she loved me anyway and went and made up a chocolate cake. Probably I didn't even notice I got no other birthday presents except a homemade cake, because I was what you'd call "hypmotized" by my sister's *Life* magazines: page after page of colored advertisements for new Chevrolets and Royal Crown Cola and Lucky Strikes and Spam. Cream of Wheat even had a colored Al Capp comic strip showing how Li'l Abner got his strength from eating a bowl of hot cereal. "Stand back, Daisy Mae," he said. The black and white pictures on every page showed the President or Veronica Lake doing something. I guess it was the pictures of war, though, that held me captive the most. I knew there was talk of war on the radio, but we didn't have a Motorola like most everybody else. I got to laying around on the floor an hour at a time, gorging my eyes with the photographs arranged on *Life's* slick pages.

The magazine's pictures of convoys of ships on the North Sea and rescues of sailors from life rafts after U-boats sunk their destroyers so fascinated me, I began to change my attitude toward the war. Though I still had a nightmare of falling bombs now and then, there was a new excitement created by the pictures. It looked like fun to be floating on a raft in the ocean and be smeared with engine oil and yanked aboard a ship's deck by sailors who'd give you a steaming cup of coffee with rum in it, whatever that was. And almost any photos of RAF night-fighters or bomber crews gave me hours of thrilling pleasure. The pictures of bomber crews always showed a half-dozen men dressed to the gills in puffy flying suits, wearing aviator caps, carrying parachute packs over their shoulders, and wearing big grins on their faces. I was persuaded. Flying Halifax bombers over the enemy was fun and adventure.

Uncle Bud walked into the room one day carrying a bucket of milk. He'd milked one of Mr. Joe Keitt's cows, the little white-faced heifer with the new calf, down at the cow shed. He hung his straw field hat on the back of a chair and carried the milk to the kitchen, where Momma would strain it through some old flour-sacking into a crock bowl and let it cool until we'd eat it with hot cornbread at supper. I never did like the taste of milk still warm from the cow. Momma did, though. She'd just lick her lips over that warm foam.

I was studying a picture of a Spitfire landing in a pasture in England when Uncle Bud came back in the room. The Spitfire had some holes in its wings the Germans had shot in it. I thought the pilot must be glad to be back on the ground and have some hot coffee with rum in it. Uncle Bud looked at the picture, too.

"I expect you heard about Ros'velt's 'secret weapon?'"

Of course, I knew about "secret weapons!" They made you think of new, powerful bombs that you'd conquer the world with. I'd seen them in comic books. Most of the time they were in the hands of evildoers.

"It ain't no secret if you know about it, Uncle Bud," I said.

"Don't many people know about it," he said. "I figured you'd want to know, being your nose in them funny books all the time." He grabbed his hat off the chair, and made to head for the door. "Better be off down to the field. It's gettin' hot out there. Lots of sun before time to go to the house."

Well, shoot, what *was* Mr. Ros'velt's "secret weapon?"

I got to my feet and followed him to the door and out on the porch. "Uncle Bud, what's that new secret weapon made out of?" I was ready to bet it was a secret gas or electric ray.

He stopped at the edge of the porch to pick up a tow sack with shelled corn in it. He flung the tow sack over his shoulder.

"Way I hear it is, Ros'velt's army men are gonna draft boys who ain't doin' nothing, only readin' funny books, then doll them up in girls' dresses and parachute them over Germany. Well, Hitler, he won't suspect them boys in pink dresses is spies finding out his secrets." Uncle Bud got one of those grins on his face like when he's pulled a fast one. "Yep, I hear Ros'velt don't cotton to the idy of you'all layin' about. I guess if I was layin' around, only my head in them funnies, I'd watch out for Ros'velt's army men."

Momma claimed Uncle Bud was always up to foolishness, no better than a kid himself, joking and pulling pranks. I could see she was right, but it didn't bother me the way it did her. For my part, you never knew when some of his story might be true, besides his joking around helped pass the time when we chopped cotton on long, hot days in the field. He was always up to something, unlike Mr. Waller, who kept his mind on getting as much work out of you as he could. His only fun was dipping Garrett's snuff.

The day after we'd moved to Calina a boy came to our yard, climbed up in the Chinaberry tree, and said his name was Bobby. He lived in the next house along the road. His daddy farmed, and owned a two-story barn near their house. They also owned a nice car.

Up in the Chinaberry tree he looked like a monkey.

"Don't thow down them Chinaberries," said Melvin Junior. "Hit somebody in the eye."

Bobby climbed down from the tree and said his mother sent him over to tell us about school, where we'd go, and all. He still looked like a big monkey, I thought, maybe because we saw him up in the tree.

"Ain't but a week left till school's out for the summer. Mother said you all have to go over to Calina and tell Mr. Cornelius you want to go to school in the fall. That way, he'll expect you're coming, and write your names on his list."

"What if I quit school and join the Army?" Melvin Junior wanted to be a soldier.

"You can't do that," said Bobby. "In the Army you have to read what it says on the boxes your bullets and all come in. All your soldiers got an education."

That being the case, the next day Melvin Junior and me walked over to Calina with Bobby so we'd get on Mr. Cornelius' list of pupils for next school year. Momma made us go and made sure we were clean when we started. Bobby had started to look less like a monkey and more like a boy, so I never thought of him in the Chinaberry tree again.

It was a long ways to walk to our new school. There wasn't any reason to be in a hurry when you had six or seven miles to go to your school. Uncle Bud called it "two dog's legs," because we walked a couple of miles one way, then took a quick left turn and walked another couple of miles, and stepped quick to the right at the Calina store, and walked a mile or so right to the Calina school. That is, if we stayed right on the road where a car whipped past every once in a while; even then, there could be adventures if you looked for them.

Bobby showed us where to cut across fields, and dodge through fences around pastures, and sneak underneath bridges, like the one we'd burn down by accident a few months later on. The countryside we walked through was typical flat-land Texas farm country: fields of cotton or corn, relieved by pastures where white-faced cows stared at us, and near the road were white frame houses standing in farm yards littered with field implements and cattle trailers. Most farm yards had a dog who'd bark, then go back and sprawl flat in the shade.

But the place on the road where Calina got its name was the most fun. On the right side of the road, going, there was a cotton gin and compress, big old wood and tin buildings, several stories high with ladders inside for climbing up to the lofts. In late summer, of course, the gin got busy sucking seeds out of the cotton, and the racket and dust made your head and ears ache. The compress was a ridged, wrinkled tin building, rusting in places where rainwater caught, standing up on wood posts high enough off the ground you could sit underneath in the dirt and eat your peanut butter sandwich before school took up. You'd see under the compress some opened sardine cans, and pieces of rusty iron, probably fell off the gin's equipment, some bottles kids had broke. None of the stuff was in anybody's way, we decided.

Scrambling out from under the compress, we could see the store. Just along the road on the other side, going, was a two-room frame store with front porch and screen door. It was Mr. J.O. Rich's store, though he was dead. Mr. Rich had two daughters who'd moved off to the town of Groesbeck and got married, one to a Womack, and Mary Beth to a Olgive, though none of this what you might call history was important to us boys. It was the penny candy and the Baby Ruths and the Co'Colas floating in the ice box that drew us through the screen doors and past the pot-belly stove, even past the post office window, directly to the big counter where local farmers stood and discussed the weather. When Mr. Rich went off and died, he was lucky to sell the store to folks who didn't mind getting trade from boys who only had nickels and pennies to spend. Lucky for us, they'd sell Lucky Strikes and Chesterfields and Brown's Mule plug-tobacco to boys.

The road turned a corner at the store, and we walked straight to Calina school, where Mr. Cornelius, the principal, enrolled me and Melvin Junior for the next school year. Mr. Cornelius wore a white shirt and dress pants and eye glasses with no frames, but he wasn't an old man like most teachers. He put me in the third grade and Melvin Junior in the fourth grade. My cursive handwriting was better than Melvin Junior's, he said. But Melvin Junior helpfully pointed out he never failed the second grade. I guess that was why Mr. Cornelius put him in the fourth grade. He said he would see me and Melvin Junior when school started in September. He kept our report cards.

"Cotton picking will be slowed down by the middle of September," he said.

On Monday morning all of us, including Momma and Mr. Waller, picked up our chopping hoes and went off to the cotton field. Momma woke me and Melvin Junior about five-thirty so we'd have some coffee and the soda biscuits she'd already baked before going to work. I got into my overalls and brogan shoes, staggered out to the toilet in the dark of morning, peed into the hole on the spiders, and went back and washed the sleep out of my eyes, ate my biscuits. We had about a half mile to walk to the field where we'd thin the cotton and chop out the early grass not yet gone to seed. By the time Mr.

Waller filed all our hoes good and sharp, it was light enough to get to work.

The rows of young cotton stretched off into the distance where mist still rose from a creek bottom. Each of us took a row, and began to shuffle along, our hoes sifting and chopping among the foot-high cotton stalks and the pushy weeds.

"Sure feels good to get some work, don't it?" Momma asked all of us who'd listen, not including me.

What I--wearing blue bib overalls, a brand new straw hat, and scuffed work shoes--didn't know at the time, me feeling the sun's heat waves begin to burn out any promise of comfort for the day, was I had started a routine which I'd follow for the next ten years of my life. Year after year I'd go to school and make friends and read some library books between early September and late May; then in the final weeks of May, I'd come home from school, eat a snack, change into my work clothes, and go to the fields for the rest of the day. By the first week of June, school and friends and books disappeared as if they never existed, replaced by full-time field work. But at the age of nine, whisking a hoe among cotton stalks, I was unprepared to wonder if I was going to do this all my life. It was just what we did. It was like cotton was king and Momma was queen, and you didn't ask questions.

The hot summer weather held on, and we worked in the fields every day of the week, plus a half day on Saturday. As a result, we made a little money chopping cotton, seventy-five cents a day. The reward me and Melvin Junior worked for was the trip to Hubbard on Saturday afternoon. We lived for the minute when Mr. Waller called out, "Quittin' time!" Momma stayed at the house on Saturday mornings, getting ready for going to town, and she'd fry a chicken for our dinner, like it was our holiday or something. After we ate dinner, Mr. Waller hitched up the mules to the wagon, then we'd all ride along the road about ten miles into Hubbard. Sometimes me and Melvin Junior would run along behind the wagon, so we could chunk clods at fence posts and such.

Mr. Waller always put up the wagon in the shade of some cottonwood trees between the East end of Main Street and the railroad tracks, where he unharnessed the mules from the wagon tongue and looped the reins around a wagon wheel. They'd rest in the shade and stamp the ground to scare off flies. Me and Melvin Junior always dashed away to the Crystal Theater, hoping to get into our seats before the lights dimmed and the cartoon and serial began. We never watched any movies except Westerns. Cowboys like Gene Autry or Tex Ritter, maybe Bob Steele or Red Ryder, provided us with adventures we re-lived all week while chopping cotton. Usually Melvin Junior would run on ahead and save seats for us at the Crystal.

One Saturday there was a wagon occupying Mr. Waller's usual shady spot. Several men and boys stood around the tail-gate of the wagon. The tail-gate had been let down, held up on both sides with chains. It was now being used as a porch for a man to stand on. Behind him the wagon held a dirty-white canvas tent, and you could see inside there was a wood cabinet like in a doctor's office which had drawers and shelves. To me it looked like the man had himself a store on wheels and a horse to pull it. In all my life in Hubbard I'd never seen the like. The spectacle of the wagon and horse at first took my attention, but the man's behavior soon struck me near dumb.

He was about the size of Mr. Waller, with a pot belly, and the oddest thing was he wore a vest, a thing I'd never seen except at the picture show. His hair was flat across his head as though he'd just took off a hat and the sweat hadn't had time to dry. I thought his face was redder than it should have been, though he could have been in the sun without his hat on. But the thing that froze my mouth open was his behavior. He was stomping backwards and forwards on his little porch, swinging some kind of handsaw. Once in a while he'd stop, stick the saw between his legs, and rat-a-tat on it with his open hand. That old saw made a whirring noise could make a person's flesh crawl. Then he took to holding the saw at both ends and bending it outwards and inwards, making the scariest sound, like: "OOOOOOEEEEEEAAAA." It must be the sound a ghost makes, I thought.

I looked at the faces of people around me, thinking they'd look scared to death, but they didn't. Some of them seemed to be enjoying the sounds like I'd enjoy listening to Gene Autry sing the Yellow Rose of Texas.

"You'all know what a saw's for, don'tcha?" The man stepped to the front of his porch and held up his handsaw. "Well, it's made for sawin.'" Then he laughed, and some of the folks laughed with him. But then he got a serious look on his face. "Some of you'all may a heard me play the saw up at the Texas state fair. Up there in Dallas. And I had many a prize come to me for playing the saw." He paused to look pleased with himself, I thought, and went on. "But I reckon they's many a leg been sawn off with this here handsaw way out on the battlefield."

I tell you when he said that I got the shivers up my back again. Somewhere up on Main Street a car horn sounded. Maybe I'm going to miss the picture show, I thought, but couldn't pull myself away.

The man pulled a chair out from the tent and set it on the porch. The next thing he said put such a fright in me, I about keeled over, especially as he seemed to be looking at me.

"I need a person come up here, let me saw off his leg."

Don't think that didn't make folks quiet down. It was like everybody in the crowd took theirselves a deep breath and didn't let it out. Quick as a calf's breath I took a peek around, see who might be crazy enough to take him up, climb up on that porch, stick their leg out, watch it drop off under that handsaw right on the porch. In my mind I could about hear it go "plunk!"

Well, I guess he thought nobody was coming up, so he began to pick on a couple of boys about Melvin Junior's age.

"I wish one a you boys was brave as I was at your age. That's what got me a medal in this man's army. Just puredee old bravery in the face of peril." He leaned out off his porch and leveled a finger at one of the boys. "Why don't you'all come up here, show these good people you ain't got no more yellow in you than's in a baboon's butt."

My whole body was stone cold, thinking what it'd be like to go up on that porch with a crazy man holding a saw. That's why I couldn't believe my eyes when one boy handed his cap to the other one, and climbed right up on the porch. A kind of hum went through the crowd, a way of everybody saying "Don't this beat all?"

The man showed the boy how he wanted him to sit on the chair and had him roll one pants leg up to the knee; then he faced the crowd and said, "Is this boy got a daddy out here?"

Nobody stepped up, so the man turned to us. He still carried that saw as if it was a tool he used every day. The boy sat on his chair, looking brave as could be. One thing I noticed about him was he wore corduroy pants and had patches on the knees. I'd never seen him around town or at school before, but Hubbard was a big place.

"On your battlefield, guns is firing every which a ways," announced the man. "Some a them bullets can tear a man's body something awful. You don't even want to talk about it. Some of you has seen it." He paused, looking at a few heads nodding in his audience. "Worst problem in the world out there is when a soldier gets a bullet hole that turns all green on him. The doctors call that gangrene." The man let that sink in. "Nothing to do but start sawin'."

The man next to me was nodding his head. I saw his lips move. I heard him say in a low voice: "Blood poison!"

"Yessir, that's your blood poison," said the man on the porch.

That's when he turned to the boy on his chair. He waved his saw in a way that would have scared the daylights out of me, and he grabbed the boy's leg with the rolled up pants and laid that cold saw blade right on the knee. I froze, and got ready to close my eyes when that leg fell off, all bloody.

But the man didn't saw just yet. I guess he wasn't ready. He put the boy's leg down and told him to set a spell. The boy didn't say a thing, just crossed his bare leg over his other knee and swung his foot back and forth. I figured he was nervous, why he done it.

Out from his hip pocket the man brought a bottle about the size of a medicine bottle, and it made me think of cough syrup Momma made me take. But it wasn't cough syrup that he held up so we could all see the bottle.

"This here is the most powerful germ killer is in the world," he explained. "Ain't nobody here ain't never had a infected sore. Maybe it was on the leg or maybe on a finger. It ain't just your soldier boy in a battle that dies a sorrowful death or gets his leg sawn off when the blood poison comes on him. I have seen the agonies of death take the life of the youth and the aged just because they neglected a fish hook in a finger or a picked-at pimple. Soon's your infection takes a hold, the blood poison's got you in its grip." The man leaned out directly at some folks right in front of the porch. "You'all know what I'm talkin' about." Some of the men nodded, but didn't say anything. I noticed there was not any women there. Probably had run off scared.

The boy had rolled down his pants leg and I thought he looked like he'd been saved because the man forgot to saw his leg. When the man saw the boy standing up, he said, "Why don't you be useful and get them bottles of germ killer out the tent. Folks is goin' to want some a that."

I watched the boy bring a cardboard box out of the tent and set it down on the porch. The box said "Vine Ripened Tomatoes, 24 Cans" on the side, but it was really full of the little bottles of germ killer. The boy stood beside the box, holding three or four bottles in his hands. I thought he looked like he might doze off to sleep just standing there. He was the bravest kid I had ever seen. Give him a medal, I figured.

But the man was busy again, whipping from one side of the porch to the other, explaining the "ninety-nine ways ever person'd use the world's most powerful germ killer," and never again have to worry about blood poison. That's if you had a bottle, he said, which cost you only two-bits, and guaranteed by the factory. Get your money back if your sores got infected. Several men near the tailgate handed up their two-bits, and the boy leaned over with their bottles.

I'd have bought a bottle for Momma, but I didn't have two bits. She gets headaches.

Chapter 12

DECEMBER 7, 1941

Many a puzzle goes through a person's head when they're in the cotton patch. It does mine. It might be the sun shining on my head all day, plus the pull of the cotton sack's strap across my shoulder and on my neck that does it to my head. But without me turning it on and off on purpose, the inside of my head hops around like a frog on dirt even while my hands are busy picking cotton out of the boles and bunching hands-full of cotton and pushing it down the mouth of the cotton sack I'm hauling behind me. It's like smack in the middle of shaking down my cotton sack, see if I got enough cotton down in there to go to the wagon to weigh up and get a drink of water, my head will start to think: "I can't do it any more. Too much heat, too much sweat, too much cotton, I can't do it." Then another part of my head says: "You ain't got no choice. Pick that cotton. Pull that sack." And it goes on like that, arguing back and forth like a man and his wife on the radio.

So it didn't surprise me or anybody else that I picked cotton through the rest of that hot summer of 1941, weighing up about a hundred pounds a day. Wasn't everybody else picking cotton? Oh, if I really thought about it, I didn't expect those college boys in *Life* magazine were picking cotton, just busy throwing their pants and shirts out some window. But it was late September when me and Melvin Junior set off for our first days at our new school in Calina, Texas, me in the third grade, Melvin Junior in the fourth.

Ever since Daddy died and me and Momma had to move away from Cottonwood school, it didn't seem like I'd learned enough at all them schools to fill a hen's tooth. Momma herself had made me recite over and over the multiplication tables, going "One times nine is nine. Nine times nine is eighty-one, I think." All those schools, though, went by faster than nine times twelve. There was Hubbard, then Union High, now at Calina, but I hadn't stayed long enough in them to remember any teachers the way I still thought about Miss Shull. Seemed like since then the only thing I'd learned was how to run faster than the mean kids who picked on us.

Right off I felt like Calina school was different. First thing was, Mr. Cornelius acted like the first man teacher I'd seen in a school who did something besides paddle the fire out of mean boys. Mr. Cornelius talked nice and was not scary, even when he came to our room and wrote on the blackboard with chalk. The boys that rode mules and horses to school still had to behave, though. It was the first time I didn't go to school in fear of my life. Not that kids couldn't make fun. Like the time my sister Lucy gave me a white navy cap with a gold anchor on it, and when I wore it to school the kids said the anchor was to hold my big ears down, keep me from flying away in the wind. But that didn't mean a thing.

Not picking cotton all day didn't mean me and Melvin Junior could sleep late and read comic books. Because Momma and them still were picking, we all got up early, ate our coffee and biscuits with Carnation condensed milk, and went off. Me and Melvin Junior and our neighbor Bobby walked five miles or more to school, depending on which fields we cut across and which bridges we smoked a grapevine under.

Our trip on the dog-leg to school became a "road to adventure" for us boys. I'd seen the words on a book at school. If you kept up on your school work, Mr. Cornelius let you sit on a chair at the back of the room and read out of some books he'd stuck up on a shelf. I liked to do that, so I kept up on my spelling and arithmetic work. And I'd found a book called "The Road to Adventure." It had a lot of poems in it about ship wrecks and snow storms and Paul Revere and so on. So that's how I got to thinking about our trip between home and school as our own "Road to Adventure."

Like the day we set that bridge on fire. Actually, we didn't so much set the bridge on fire as we set the sea cane on fire and it jumped onto the bridge. We never intended for the wood bridge to get burned. It was a gully underneath the bridge, and that's where we dragged some stalks from a big stand of sea weed, growing higher than our heads. Intending to smoke cut-off stems for our "cigarettes," we built a fire of dried leaves, and poked the stems in the flames. Gray smoke swirled up from the fire, making us stand back with our lighted sea canes. Soon me and Melvin Junior and Bobby were sucking heavy smoke through the "cigarettes."

"This here's as good as roll-your-own," announced Melvin Junior, coughing a little bit in the smoke cloud rising from the fire.

"Bet you all can't let smoke come out your nose," said Bobby. He slowly leaked white smoke from both nostrils. It was a good trick. I was going to give her a try, but was interrupted before I could drag on my stem.

"Bridge on fire!" shouted Melvin Junior, jumping around like water drops on a hot stove.

Sparks from the fire had landed in the rotted underside of several bridge planks, and flames were inching along the boards. We scrambled up the sides of the gully onto the road. We saw smoke leaking between the boards where nails had come loose.

"Get some water from that tank!" yelled Bobby, pointing across the road.

There was a stock tank in the pasture beyond a bob-wire fence. We threw our books and satchels down beside the road, and ducked between the wires. But what would we carry water in? We ran toward the tank, yelling. Several rusty tin cans lay about near the tank dam as if somebody had emptied trash, and we grabbed them up and splashed into the water.

I ran back toward the bridge with two cans, but both were rusty and leaking. I splashed some water as I ducked under the bob-wire. When I got to the fire, I saw most of my water had been wasted, but I sprinkled the flames and headed back to the tank.

"Here comes somebody," called Melvin Junior.

A car pulling a trailer pulled up beside the bar ditch, and a farmer I didn't know got out. He saw what was happening, and pulled a tow sack out of the trailer and began to beat out the fire. Soon only wisps of smoke leaked through the boards. Melvin Junior and Bobby stood at the side of the road, each holding a rusty can leaking water.

The man wiped the back of his hand across his forehead and adjusted his hat.

"Don't it beat all how dry that sea cane got this summer?" he said.

My cursive writing was so good I wrote letters to my sister Lucy who claimed she read them. And I didn't mind reading anything, even bringing books from the school cloak room for reading at home, especially the books with stories that used a picture somebody drew with a ink pen and put some pink and yellow on the people before they finished. Then Mr. Cornelius one day complimented me on my multiplication tables, said I was "exempt" from the big arithmetic test because I knew it all. What that meant was while other kids wrote and erased and sweated on their papers, I put my feet under my desk and read any book I wanted to. I guess that was Big-Head important, because I overheard Momma bragging to a neighbor, "Leon is exempt!" I knew she was proud.

I'd reached the place where I learned nobody ever told me anything that wasn't about multiplication tables or spelling. Take the Japanese, for example. I calculated everybody but me knew what they were up to. Not me, though. Nobody ever let me in on a thing until after it took place. That's why I was in the yard figuring to make me a real Christmas tree the Sunday morning the Japanese attacked Pearl Harbor with their airplanes. Nobody in my family had ever thought of cutting down a tree and sticking lights on it and calling it a "Christmas tree." I guess Momma, Mr. Waller, and them had always thought if you cut down a tree, you put it in the stove, lit it, baked some biscuits. But I'd seen in a comic book that folks out in the world, they'd chop down a tree, sprinkle glitter stuff on it, and call it a Christmas tree, which looked a good idea to me. In the comic book they seemed to get more presents that way. So I was looking for a tree little enough to bring in our house and decorate it and make Melvin Junior and them think of what the newspapers called "the Christmas season."

It must have been about the time I was whacking a branch off a peach tree in the yard was when a wave of torpedo bombers surprised the Navy ships anchored in the deep water at Pearl Harbor. In the next several days I'd read in the newspapers we borrowed from neighbors about the giant battleships torpedoed and bombed before they knew what was up. Of course, it was Sunday morning after all. Who would expect? You'd think the Japanese would be in church. But in a few days Mr. Cornelius explained to us at school how it was earlier over there than it was in Calina. We never knew that.

Mr. Cornelius also told us how American battleships were named for states. That helped us to understand why the newspapers showed pictures of sinking and burning ships with names like USS *West Virginia*, USS *Oklahoma*, and USS *Arizona*. The newspapers also told how many hundreds of sailors died in the attack and in the water. There was even oil all over the water. In some of the pictures you could see a sailor in a white uniform firing his machine gun straight up at a red ball on the fuselage of a dive bomber screaming out of the clouds while a thousand red-hot machine gun bullets riddled the head of the old Jap pilot and he fell out in a parachute.

The next day, on Monday, everybody was mad as a hornet at the "Japs," as they got to be called. I'd never heard it before, though I'd admit I didn't know many people from Japan. You'd hear people say things like "Japs is cowards. They sneak up behind your back." But Uncle Bud, who knew about the army by nearly being drafted, put it straight: "The Japs have got it coming to them now, you wait and see." I expect that's exactly what they meant later on when people'd say, "Remember Pearl Harbor!" You'd see it in the papers and hear it on the radio.

On Monday me and Melvin Junior and Bobby talked about dive bombers and battleships all the way to school. It was exciting to think about, not knowing when we'd be surprise attacked ourselves. We made us a plan to dive into a bar ditch if a Zero aimed a bomb at us. When we got to school, we found out we were going to listen to President Franklin Roosevelt make a speech about Pearl Harbor. Mr. Cornelius said we'd go across the road to the Methodist church and have the radio on. And that's what we done. Sure enough, somebody had put a big Motorola on a table and it was plugged into a socket beside the electric light. The church had big windows the way a church will do. Still, it was kind of dark in the big room. All the furniture was dark, too, and smelled like it had been polished by the preacher. Us kids filed into the church and lined ourselves onto the polished, wooden benches. Mr. Cornelius said they were "pews," and we should be quiet.

"This is a church, and there may be a star spangled banner," he said quietly.

There was some talking like whispers on the radio, then some music and we put our hands over our shirt pockets.

"The President of the United States of America," somebody said on the radio.

It made you kind of sad listening to the President of the United States. His voice made him sound like a great man. He was sad, too, and while he spoke you couldn't imagine laughing or scooting around on the pew. I thought about how I felt when Mama got to carrying on about my daddy dying. Maybe that's how all things sad make a person feel.

President Roosevelt told us about what happened yesterday when the Japanese airplanes sneaked an attack on the battleships at Pearl Harbor in Hawaii. You could tell he hated to do it, but he said he'd asked the Congress in Washington, D.C. to declare war on Japan. He called them an "Empire," which made you think about history. That made it official, and we were all at war with the Japs. The President of the United States said from now on he would call December 7, 1941, "a day of infamy." That was yesterday, and we'd always have to call it that from now on, whatever an "infamy" was. Mr. Cornelius would know.

Momma was carrying on when me and Melvin Junior got home from school. She'd heard that a war was on, and she'd been afraid the Japanese might attack us right away. She'd wanted to come over to school and get me and Melvin Junior. You never knew how soon those Japanese bombers would fly over here to Calina and make a mess of things. I heard that Mrs. Powell across the road had talked some sense into Momma, got her to wait for us to walk home. That night she put sheets up over several windows, "black-outs," she called them, for she'd heard they were doing that in Los Angeles, California.

"Don't let the Japs see you're home," she said.

Pearl Harbor was the most exciting thing I could ever recall. Of course, I wanted to catch up on anything we'd missed by not being at Pearl Harbor in Hawaii on Sunday. If you're not there when a war starts, you have to watch and listen to any and all survivors. Because we didn't have a radio or take a daily newspaper, I'd get a little news here, a piece of news there. Mostly rumors about the Japs going on attack wherever you'd find them. I was the most excited I'd ever been, I tell you. Worst was, I had to wait two or three weeks for a *Life* magazine to fall in my hands. I began to think we'd whip the Japs before I got my hands on the full story in *Life* magazine, but finally, Mr. Cornelius brought a copy to school we could look at. It had a picture of the American flag on the cover. That was all. The wind was waving the flag, but you could count its forty-eight stars.

Inside *Life* there was a picture of the United States Congress listening to the President tell them it was a day of infamy. Every seat in the place was taken! Everybody was wearing a new suit it looked like, and every man was paying attention. One thing that caught my eye in the picture was a big clock on the wall back behind President Roosevelt's head. The clock's hands said it was twenty minutes until one o'clock. That made me feel funny, because I knew when somebody set up their camera and took that picture at just at that time I was sitting in the Methodist church to hear Mr. Roosevelt speak on the radio. It made me feel like I was right there.

Life magazine put a guide in the magazine showing how you could tell a Jap if you met one coming toward you. You could tell he was not a Chinaman because a person from China was tall and handsome like a movie star, but a Jap was short and squatty and had squinch eyes. *Life* showed you pictures of a Jap and a Chinaman, and you could tell the difference and call a FBI G-man.

But Christmas was coming, and me and Melvin Junior couldn't spend all our time on the new war. I had to finish my Christmas tree, a job you'd never think would take day and night. I'd learned that a tree would not get in the house. So I had to make do with a peach tree branch.

"Don't this look like a Christmas tree?" I asked Melvin Junior.

"I guess I've seen about a hund'erd Christmas trees," said Melvin Junior. "What you've got there looks more like a bush."

I trimmed the lowest twigs off, which made the branch resemble a midget tree. I found a board in the hen house off a crate Momma used to keep hen's scratch in. It was about the size of a Sears catalog, only not as thick.

"Guess I'll nail my tree on this board, keep it standing up."

"You'll split that air board with a ten penny nail," said Melvin Junior. "It looks rotten to me."

I was careful and nailed the branch to the board with three or four nails, bent over.

"I saw a Texaco calendar once had a Christmas tree covered a foot deep in snow," allowed Melvin Junior. "They ain't no snow in a thousand miles of here."

Since Melvin Junior was right about that, I went out in the cotton patch behind the barn. The cotton stalks were dead, fallen over with dried up leaves and empty burrs touching the ground. I knew there were dried-up burrs with little bitty cotton sticking out. I found some dirty cotton still on the dead stalks, pulled it out, and shook out the dirt and carried it to my tree.

Melvin Junior studied the cotton. "Ain't nobody going to believe that cotton is snow," said Melvin Junior. "That's what I'd call fake snow. It won't fool nobody. They'll say, 'Leon's been out in the field pulling boles.'"

After I laid the cotton around the foot of my Christmas tree, I had to go and round up some decorations, which we didn't have.

"I have seen maybe a hund'erd Christmas trees, and they all had lighted candles on them," said Melvin Junior. "You burn the house down."

So I put my mind to it and found some sticks of chewing gum wrapped in tin foil, and found that tin foil was good for covering nickels and pennies. I hung them with string on my Christmas tree for decorations. I put it up on a table and showed it to Momma who said it was fine.

"You ain't got a single present under that Christmas tree," allowed Melvin Junior. "I put my money on Santa Claus."

Of course, he was right. I didn't know what to do for presents for a long time. Then I got an idea. One night I stayed up later than anybody and kept the coal oil lamp on so I could see what I was doing. I got some Sunday comic pages, in color, and I scissored out some wrapping paper. For Momma I drew a Christmas card with Crayolas and I put it in a little match box, and wrapped it in a comic page and tied it with some colored string. It had the look of a Christmas present and I put it under my tree. There was no present for me, but I knew what I'd do. The Christmas back at Union High, I'd got a Texan cap pistol, one with a pearl-handled steer head on the grip. It had fancy scroll work on the barrel and I had kept it safe, because I really loved it. Why wouldn't it make a good Christmas present again? I took and wrapped it in the colored comic paper, signed a little piece of paper: "To Leon for Christmas." I put it under my Christmas tree. I had to admit it looked kind of funny, being nearly as big as the tree, but you can't have rules the way the Post Office does about the size of your presents.

Chapter 13

A HANT'S MARBLE

I was up on the thresher with an umbrella ready to jump off. Momma stood down below, wringing her hands in her print apron, and hollering up at me.

"Leon, get down from there. You break your neck, and then where'd we be?" She took a step toward the thresher. "We need to get a move on and pack up so Papa and them can load the wagon after dinner." She moved to go to the house, but stopped and turned back. "Don't you'all want to get over yonder to Mr. David's place?"

Melvin Junior stood in back of Momma, thinking, "Jump! Jump!" I could read his face.

How I came to be up on the big old Allis Chalmers threshing machine with Momma's umbrella was I'd seen a navy aircraft carrier in a *Wings* comic book, to my mind resembling a threshing machine plowing through the ocean. The Allis Chalmers thresher itself had the look of a war-wagon. It stood on four iron wheels, supporting a box-like metal tank with a flat-top roof. Several pulley-wheels attached to the side of the thresher were looped by heavy belts that slapped and whupped like a giant sewing machine when it was up and running. A movable tin spout on the back end gun- threshed oats into a wagon if you pulled up underneath. There was a handy ladder on the side so you could climb up on top of the machine. It seemed natural, then, to climb up on top of the aircraft carrier and parachute off. Melvin Junior agreed.

Sure, I wanted to move over to Mr. David's place. The Hickman Ranch, as Mr. Waller called it. We'd be moving back to the place where I was born. Me and Momma had moved away to Hubbard after Daddy died, then roamed all over creation, boarding with family. Now, here I was, ten years old, and in the fifth grade, all ready to go back where I'd started from a long time ago. Mr. Waller and Uncle Bud talked to Mr. David in the First State Bank at Hubbard, and he wanted us to move on the place and work for him.

What I'd thought a daring adventure while dragging the parachute up the ladder to the top of the aircraft carrier now looked more like a terrifying leap off a two-story farm machine, with a long fall through space and a hard landing on the path to the chicken coop. Looking over the rim of my flat-top roost on the thresher, I could see chicken scratchings on the hard earth sprinkled with pebbles and chicken do. It seemed a long way down. But I did have the umbrella.

"Am I got to climb up there and give you a shove?" Melvin Junior was losing patience.

I popped open Momma's umbrella. Black silk cloth stretched tight over metal stays that looked like spokes in a wheel. When I pushed it open, there was a click, so you'd know it was open for good. The umbrella's handle ended in a crook like a goose neck. My parachute was open and ready for jumping. I stepped to the lip of the carrier's deck and lifted my parachute above my head.

"If I float off toward the stock tank, chase and grab me," I called to Melvin Junior.

Without even picking a landing site, I closed both eyes and leapt into space.

In comic books the shot-down aviators always descend slowly after they slide the cowling back and parachute from their smoking, spinning fighter planes. You can see them tugging on the chute lines so as to direct their landing away from German machine gun nests. In my plunge off the carrier I had no time to watch out for the enemy. I fell so fast I only heard my parachute snap and warp wrong-side-out, then I hit the ground.

You know how it feels to run fast as you can go through a dark room and forget a door is closed? I guess that's how I felt when I landed. Stunned. Wind knocked out of me, all I could do was lie on my back and try to get a breath. Only thing I could do was check my finger nails, see if I was dead. Slowly, my mind began to invent questions out of nothing. Would it hurt if I stood up? How would I keep Momma from knowing what happened? What was Melvin Junior hollering about?

"Get up! Get up! Your parachute didn't work that time. You got to do it again!"

I did manage to get up, but I wasn't about to do it again. I felt kind of sick, but I walked around some and nothing was broken. Except Momma's umbrella.

"Put it in the grass behind the hen house," said Melvin Junior. "Aunt Bill's busy packing up, and she'll just think she accidently left her umbrella behind."

By that evening the wagon with sideboards was loaded. All Momma'd left out was glasses and spoons so we'd have hot cornbread and cool sweetmilk for our supper, maybe some coffee next morning before we left. The kitchen stove with its coal-oil jug would have to stay behind, wait for Mr. Waller and Uncle Bud to come back for it and the wood ice box.

Most people wouldn't think riding on top of a wagon loaded with old furniture and pulled by two mules was worth talking about. I expect they'd been riding in Fords and hadn't done it. You can have a lot of fun up on a wagon. There's time to see everything you ride past. Always in the sky you'll see four or five dark buzzards, not even flapping their wings, but just circling lazy-like as if all they had to do was study about the ground below. Any time there's a farm house beside the road, a couple of farm dogs, usually a collie and a shepherd, jump off the porch and race like mad dogs to the end of their yard, and a woman comes around the corner of the house and calls, "Hey, you'all, dogs," and they wag their tails and go back. Most times in a wagon you see a snake on the road, a grass snake or a chicken snake, maybe a black coach whip, sometimes dead in a car rut, flies buzzing, but other times if you're lucky a live snake, long as a calf rope, slithers into the grass beside the road, and you see its tail disappear and you shiver nice and good.

Me and Melvin Junior found the best fun was getting out of the wagon and running along beside or back of it, close enough you can hear the wheel rims crunching the gravel. That way, we'd chunk rocks at fence posts, sometimes at Dr. Pepper bottles somebody lost out of their car on the way home. Since mules didn't go fast as a car, we'd go down in a gully or creek and look for crawdads, then run and catch up with the wagon. One time we found a fine old terrapin moseying along in the bar ditch, and we caught him and took him in the wagon for a ride until Momma made us put him down again. She said he'd get home. He was yellow and shiny on his bottom shell as if he'd been polished at the shoe parlor.

I can't tell you who was happier being back on Mr. David's place, me or Momma. You might have thought Momma, because she cried. "We're going to be back where we lived with Daddy." I guessed she'd carry on, but that was about it. She'd remember how she took me and we moved off the place because she couldn't farm like a man, but now we had Mr. Waller and Uncle Bud, plus me and Melvin Junior, to do a man's work. Probably I was most happy, though, because I felt like we'd never, ever have to move again. Which I was dang tired of. Maybe I'd grow up here and be done with it.

Uncle Bud was sitting on a box of something or other, and he was wearing new overalls he'd bought for moving day. He'd noticed a cotton field, so he said to Momma, "Bill, I hope you all brought Leon and Melvin Junior's cotton sacks. They can't wait to get out in that cotton patch." He was teasing.

"We ain't got cotton on our minds," I said. "We'll be off in them trees looking for some squirrels."

"You all better watch out down in them bottoms. Squirrels like nuts. They might hide you boys in a holler tree."

The biggest surprise in the world come when we got to the house we'd all live in. Mr. Waller's mule team pulled our wagon-load of furniture right up in the yard of a two-story house, and he said "Whoa." It looked so deserted it give me a scare at first, then a thrill, because we'd never lived in a house with upstairs, and with any mind at all you could imagine what's up there. The house just set there and stuck up in the air. A porch with an overhang went across nearly the front of the house. Way up over that porch was two windows like eyes. I knew a stairs would be inside so you'd get up there and spy out over the country. If you had a spy-glass, you'd see anything.

We all walked inside the house to look around before Mr. Waller and Uncle Bud moved our belongings in. The empty front room echoed our footsteps as if we were in a haunted house. Momma hated to see the house had been used to store hay, which left straw and chaff in the corners of the front room. Somebody had thrown a Sears catalog on the floor, with pages ripped out, likely for the toilet out back among the trees. She'd have to clean up the floors before anything was set up.

"I'd expected we'd move into the big house," she said, looking around and kicking at the straw on the floor. "I didn't know we'd be stuck down here in a hay shed." It sounded like Mr. Waller hadn't explained everything to Momma before we moved. Sometimes he didn't.

Mr. Waller stood in the door, looking in and getting ready to spit snuff all over, if Momma didn't watch out. "Elmer Morgan's wife and kids is up there in the big house," he said. "He's off in the war sommers." He leaned out the door and spit brown snuff on something, then turned back in. "David said she'd stay there while the Morgans found her a place."

I went back outside to find Melvin Junior standing near a bob-wire fence, looking over a big sandy field close to our front yard that

191

stretched way off to a line of post oaks and bois d'arc brush. Shadows of clouds moved over the sandy field.

"They's enough dang goat-heads and grass burrs out there to make you wear shoes," he said.

Behind the house was a stand of post oaks and mesquite. "Likely to be some dang prickly pears in there, too," I suggested. Melvin Junior just looked, because he was figuring out where we'd investigate our new home.

"You ever sleep in a attic?" he wanted to know.

"No, I ain't," I said. "You?"

"I guess a million or more," he answered. "But we better look up there before Aunt Bill gets rousting that hay around with her broom."

The stairs to the loft was off the front room, going right up with a banister to hold on to and not fall. It got dark at the top and you wished you had a coal-oil lantern.

At the top of the steps I stared through the dark at a wide, open room, more like a barn loft than a place you'd sleep in. One regular-size window let in some light. The funniest thing was the ceiling sloped down so you had to hunker if you walked over to the walls except for the front and back ones. I walked to the window and looked out. From up here those moving clouds that made shadows looked even closer. I saw a sandy road that ran along a fence and disappeared in the woods beyond the field with the grass burrs. I wondered where that road went.

"Come see this," Melvin Junior called from the back of the room.

He was squatted down, looking at something. I was afraid it would be a dead mouse or some such to scare us in the loft. He was pointing at the floor.

There set a marble.

It was an old-timey crock marble, big around as a two-bit piece, brown like pie dough, with several tiny pits as if somebody stuck it with a pin when the clay was still moist.

"Finder's keepers, loser's weepers," said Melvin Junior. He picked up the marble and held it in his hand.

I said, "You know what this means?"

"What?"

"It means somebody was up here," I said.

Melvin Junior looked at me. "That is the dumbest thing I ever heard," he said. "How in the tar would a marble get up here? You figure it flew in the winder like a pigeon?"

"No, dumb-nut. What I mean is it's so old it had to belong to somebody old, maybe like a pioneer fighting the Indians, maybe way back to George Washington."

I touched the marble in his hand. He closed his fist around the marble.

"Why'd George Washington ever be in Texas?"

"Maybe not George Washington," I said. "But what I mean is, that marble's old as the hills. It might'ave been lost up here by the ghost of some ancient old codger."

There was a minute when it got real quiet, and I could hear only Melvin Junior breathe. I was holding my own breath. It was dark and quiet in the loft.

"Finder's keepers...," Melvin Junior started to speak.

"If a hant left this marble up here, we better not move it," I said.

Melvin Junior got up and walked over to the window with his marble. He held it up to the light and closed one eye and studied it, turning it one way, and another. He couldn't see through it, because it was a crock marble.

"If this is a hant's marble, it might have powers," he said, and put it in his pocket.

I saw I wasn't going to talk any sense into his head, so we went back down the stairs.

There wasn't any reason for us to hang around while Uncle Bud and Mr. Waller moved us in the house. Only thing for us to do was explore. You know what it's like to be set down in a new place. There's a mystery around every corner. You can't do like a cat in a new place, just hide under the bed. So me and Melvin Junior lit out back down the road we come in on, where we'd seen a barn and a stock tank. The road was sandy and there could be sandburrs, but we were wearing shoes.

The barn wasn't nothing we hadn't seen before. Some hay bales nearly filled one room by the cow pen, some bridles and horse collars hanging on nails on the wall. Several stalls for cows or horses ran along the opposite side of the barn, where feed bins mostly held straw. For a barn, it was more like a shed with tack for horses, but with no horses.

Standing on the board fence of the cow pen, we could see the tank, which looked like a better place to investigate. We walked on down to the tank and climbed up on the dam which ran most all the way around the pond. There was enough water you could pretend it was a lake. The water was dirty, probably from cows peeing in it, but there was some green moss and lily pads around the edges. We knew there'd be frogs hiding in there. We chunked a rock, and frogs hopped into the water like a handful of airgun BBs.

From the other direction on the road came the rackety sound of a motor. We watched, and pretty soon a red Farmall tractor turned the corner, coming right by the tank dam. The red color had faded to orangish, giving the tractor a hardworking look. It was my favorite kind of tractor, the one I wanted to drive when I got bigger. They called it a "tricycle" Farmall. They called it that because it had two smaller wheels angled together like a V in front and two bigger wheels, one either side of the driver's seat, turning behind a fender so you wouldn't be grabbed by the wheel. The tractor's steering wheel was on a long rod, running past the exhaust pipe, which put out a loud popping sound that sounded grand. Driving a Farmall made you feel grownup.

Up in the driver's seat of the Farmall was one of the Morgan boys, whose family lived around the corner of the road. Mr. Morgan was kind of old, and he had a handful of kids, both boys and girls, all of them older than me. Wilmer was the oldest brother. Elmer and Delmer were the other boys, and Delmer, the youngest, had give me trouble when I'd wanted to play with the rubber guns they made to play cowboys and Indians down on the creek. I had an idea in my head that somehow Mr. Morgan and his family were related to Melvin Junior, but he didn't say. I'd have to find out later on. They all worked for Mr. David, like us.

The driver stopped beside the dam and cut the motor. He didn't have on overalls like Uncle Bud would have wore. Instead, he wore a pair of khaki pants and a dress shirt so old it looked like a castoff. And his hat was a fedora type, but sweat stains were around the hatband as though the owner of the hat worked hard. Maybe the hard work was also the reason he was thin and kind of bent over, even on the tractor.

"Hidey," he said. "I'm Wilmer Morgan. I guess you boys with Mr. Waller. You all get moved in?"

"About," said Melvin Junior. "They go back to Mr. Keitt's tomorrow for the stove."

"Momma's sweeping out the hay," I said.

Wilmer grinned. "I expect Mr. David forgot to tell you'all it's been a hay shed ever since Arlo and Mildred moved out." He took off his stained hat, inspected it, put it back on. "Well, I better go tell Mr. Waller if you all need anything, let us know." He shifted into gear, and the tractor started popping again. Dark smoke let out of the exhaust pipe. "You boys watch out for them water moccasins, now," he called above the racket.

Water moccasins? Boy, we'd heard about them snakes, about if it was a cottonmouth you could see their mouth all sickly white inside before they stab their keen teeth in you and pump you so full of poison you'd bloat up and drown in the water.

"What's that black thing sticking up there in the water?" Melvin Junior pointed, directing my sight to a dark object like the end of a stick, poking out of the water. Was it moving?

"I bet it's a moccasin," I said, straining to see.

"I'd like to know if they jump out on the land," said Melvin Junior. "Maybe the next time we come to the tank we better tote a stick."

That night I was trying to go to sleep in our new house. I thought about our first day back on the Hickman ranch. We'd rode on a wagon load of furniture and moved into a two-story house. In the dark attic right now up over our heads, Melvin Junior'd found a marble left behind by a hant. But most of all, there was a wet, black cottonmouth moccasin, bloated with hateful poison, lurking over the dam, in the waters of our stock tank.

Chapter 14

NO HOPE AT NEW HOPE

If you'd stand on the dam of the stock tank, the one full of poison snakes, and look all around, ever which way you looked, it would be the Hickman Ranch, as Mr. Waller called it. That was how much cow pasture and cotton patch and creek bottom Mr. David owned. Momma explained to me one time how Mr. David's daddy had come to Texas from somewheres and hauled out his checkbook whenever he'd light on a part of Hill County nobody wanted anymore. By the time his daddy died and was buried in the Hubbard cemetery, he owned a mighty big chunk of the county, and Mr. David claimed the place, and he farmed and ranched out of his big house in Waco. That explained how we got to live on the Hickman Ranch.

I felt kind of proud living on Mr. David's place, what with all the fields, and meadows, and creek bottoms. You could roam all over the land, see big old oak and pecan and mulberry trees, and gaze up at the dark-blue sky going from one end to the other. Clouds sometimes ambled across that blue sky like cat tail fuzz in a water trough. Other times it was low black clouds rumbling with thunder. You'd be right out in the Texas weather without any cover. There was a lot of other people lived on the place, everybody working like us.

I remember the day I told about when Wilmer Morgan drove the red Farmall tractor up to the tank dam. Well, around the corner of that road was the Carraway house. It wasn't so much a house as it was a log cabin, but a really big one, left over from the old days. Mr. Carraway's family lived in the house that was one time a station on the long road between Dallas and Austin, the capital of Texas. Back then, the roads might be muddy, the bridges over flooded, and the Comanches mad as red ants. The cabin was made out of split logs, every one of which fitted the other ones in notches cut out with axes like if Abraham Lincoln had done it. From out in the yard it looked like two cabins patched together by a porch, and between the two cabins was a windy open space everybody called a dog-run. They said you could run a hound dog right through the house if you wanted to. Back in the olden days, the folks who rode horses down to Austin might stop at the station, rest the horses, and have a pot of coffee and corn bread. That's why they called it a way station. Now it was the place where the Carraways lived with their kids, and Mr. Carraway cut everybody's hair of a Sunday.

The Morgan place was along the same road just a little ways, then across a dry creek, and set among big oak trees. Mr. Morgan's house was a rattle-trap, plain board dwelling for his family, set up on sawed logs with room under the porch and house for dogs to sleep out of the sun. I liked Missus Morgan and her daughter, Frances, a large woman, which me and Melvin Junior visited and set on the porch while they lay back in rocking chairs and dipped snuff with sticks off peach branches. They both gossiped about everybody's business but their own. Missus Morgan was nice to us, though she had one arm wouldn't work as a lightening bolt had come through the kitchen window during a thunder storm and struck her fork she was eating her supper with. The Morgan boys, only Wilmer and Delmer now at home with Elmer off fighting in the war, worked in the fields and at the big red barn. Around back of their house there was a car tire hanging from a oak tree on a rope, which you could swing round and round on until you got sick and throwed up. A barn and corral was across the road.

Walk up along the road and you'd come to the big tank and the big red barn. The big tank was for cows to water, the water kept back of the biggest dirt dam I'd seen. The water was chock full of catfish and perch and turtles and water moccasins. You could fish if you dug up a can of worms, didn't care what you caught. Oftentimes, Missus Morgan and Frances would set on the dam and put a worm on a hook and throw it out in the water with their sea cane fishing poles. Aunt Mildred was bad about spending half a day on the dam, throwing her line in, and pulling out them catfish. It made you wish you'd be there in her kitchen when she fried them up in a hot skillet and give you a glass of sweet iced tea. One end of the tank was deep, but the water near the road was shallow enough my daddy, when I was little, would drive the mules and wagon through the water to make the wood wheels on the wagon swell up against their iron rims. I'd still remember looking over the side of the wagon and seeing us out in the tank, water under us, like being on a ship at sea. At the deep end of the tank, over back of the dam, was a place Uncle Wylie said he'd seen a ghost one time that guarded buried treasure.

If you peeled off in the other direction you'd come to the red barn, so big you'd see it from near about anywheres on the Hickman Ranch, like it was on a hill. Say you were up in a mulberry tree, eating the juicy black-purple berries, hanging tight to a limb at the same time, your fingers stained purple. Maybe you'd happen to look through the branches, and you'd say, "The big red barn's got the sun on it." See, the tin roof reflected like a mirror. But you knew under that tin roof was a loft filled to the rafters with bales of hay, ripe and ready for Mr. David's cows when winter feeding started. Part of the big red barn was the corral and the loading chutes where his steers got put on the trucks to go to the stock sales in Hubbard.

A road peeled out of the red barn lot and went through a plank gate and loped out across the fields straight as a arrow, plowed furrows and rounded terraces on both sides, then popped up a slight hill and drove right into the yard of the house I was born in. If you followed me, you'd just about made a complete circle, starting at the two-story house where I lived now, and ended up where I'd got my start over ten years ago. Come to think about it, that's a mystery. The house looked the same as I'd remember. It's what folks will call "weather beat." There's a front yard, divided in two by a single bob wire. A cedar tree grows beside the porch. It's the one I climbed up while my daddy died in the front room of the house way back there, another mystery.

It being too late in the fall for me and Melvin Junior to pick cotton, we had to get to our new school. Momma had Uncle Bud walk with us through the pin oak and mesquite woods on the other side of the sand field in front of our house. Nobody knew what all was in there. It turned out the main road was at the house where the Pasleys lived. Mr. Albert Pasley worked for Mr. David like us, and his wife, Geneva, and him had a girl named Delores, who went to school, too. When we come to the main road, we climbed over a bob wire gate and stood there. Uncle Bud said, "Either one of you'all know which a ways is Dallas?"

"It's back off that way," said Melvin Junior, pointing kind of where we lived.

"Well, don't go that way or you'all end up in Dallas. Nobody'd ever find you." He laughed, and pointed up the road in the other direction and said, "You'all follow this road 'till you come to the end of it, and that's your school." Then he up and walked off and left us in the road.

New Hope school was a two-room house, not that it looked like a school any more than our two-story house did. It was painted white and had a well in the front yard with a cover over it so little kids wouldn't go head over heels in it. At the end of the back yard was a church building, not much different from our school house, except it had pigeons roosting in a steeple. The girls had a toilet not far from the church, and it looked like anybody wanted to could use it on Sunday. What was so funny, though, was the boys didn't have a toilet, which meant we had to cross the main road and go down across a field to the tree-lined creek to pee. I learned sometimes they'd pee before they got to the creek.

Inside the New Hope school house was where we set in our desks all in a row. Each pupil had a desk made up of a folding seat and a nice, oak-colored wood table top decorated with a hole to keep your ink bottle in and pupils' initials and names carved with knives and ten-penny nails. Underneath the desk top was a shelf to hold your books and lunch sacks and any toys such as Barlow knives, bags of marbles, or distributor caps off old cars. A pot-belly coal stove sat in a corner like it had been told to behave.

Our teacher, Miss Griffin, was small and young, and cut her hair short. She wasn't even married. Usual thing she'd wear a print dress from the Sears catalog and ugly old-person's shoes. She was in charge of grades one to seven, which seems like a lot but since there'd be only two or three pupils in each grade it was nothing to brag about. What she'd do was she'd have three or four little kids up front to recite their spelling, while the rest of us worked lessons at our desks. Usual thing, though, truth to tell, was Miss Griffin had more trouble with the boys working at their desks than with the pupils reciting up front. This is where the trouble begins. Some of the sixth and seventh grade boys had growed up big on their mothers' cooking at supper and ugly on their daddies' working in the fields, where they'd rather be than in school. You'd know most of them had failed their grades before. I could never figure out who'd want them to be educated.

Miss Griffin didn't have any ways to scare them, and she needed some ways bad. She was too little and too young. Besides these problems, Miss Griffin had a brother being tortured in a Japanese concentration camp. You couldn't mention it. If you did, she'd cry. Some of the big boys would say, "Miss Griffin, tell us about your brother and the Japs." That would set her off, and she'd set at her desk and cry into a handkerchief while the little kids looked scared.

Me and Melvin Junior had started late here at New Hope, so we didn't know at first "the lay of the land." We expected to play ball or Red Rover at recess, something like that. But the other boys all took off for a ditch on the other side of the road from the school house, and we did too, except we didn't know what kind of game it was.

"You'all pile up some clods and rocks over there," said one bigger boy.

"Pick the biggest ones you can throw," said another boy.

All us boys went up and down the ditch that ran alongside the main road where it turned off to go to Hubbard one way and Penelope the other way, searching for big rocks, some round, some knobby, and we stacked them in piles.

"That's enough," said one big boy. "Recess be over before you know it."

"You new boys line up here in the ditch and prepare for firing," said another boy, looking at me.

I got a round rock in each hand. Throwing rocks was always fun. I didn't know what we were supposed to throw at, surely not at each other, they were too big for comfort.

One boy faced the school house and called out, "Ready, aim, fire!"

Every boy started throwing rocks hard as can be at the school house! Rocks pounded on the roof, along the sides of the house, down on the porch. The sound was louder than any hail storm you ever lived through.

The leader boy shouted, "Give hell to ole lady Griffin!"

I wasn't throwing, because I thought what would Momma do if she found out I was throwing rocks at the teacher.

When the pounding on the school house let up, Miss Griffin put her head out the door and called out, "All you boys stop that and come in. Recess is over." When we got inside I could tell by her face she was mad or scared.

I set in my desk and looked around. Some of the little kids and the girls looked scared too. But the big boys, like seventh graders, were grinning really big. They sprawled in their desks, their clod-hopper shoes sticking in the aisles as if they wanted to trip somebody. I tell you, I hadn't ever seen anything like this New Hope school in my life.

Miss Griffin stood behind her desk, sort of like in a fort, and struck the desk with a ruler. She was mad and red in the face. "I've told you boys before, and I'm telling you again. If you don't behave and stop throwing rocks at the school, I'm going to get your parents in here."

One of the seventh-grade boys who'd played the leader in the ditch, a tall boy with lots of dark hair needed cutting, and a few pimples on his face, and looked to be too old for seventh grade, put up his hand like he wanted to go to the toilet.

"Yes, Nugene. What do you want?"

"Miss Griffin, you goin' to have your brother come straighten us boys out?"

There was giggling among the big boys at their seats.

I couldn't imagine what she would do. I guess she was too mad to cry. Instead, she came over to Nugene's desk and stood beside him, looking right in his dark, pimpled face. I was afraid what would happen next, because he was bigger than she was, plus mean.

"Nugene, I've put up with all I can from you. I'm dismissing you from class. You get your books and go home. Don't you come back to school until next Monday. If you show up before then, I'm having the school board on you and your daddy." She stood there while he grabbed a book from his desk, and jumped up like a mad rooster. It scared me, because I thought he might hit the teacher. Still, he just turned and stomped out. Everything got so quiet in the room.

I'd never thought the fifth grade at New Hope would be hard for me. I'd been used to reading books in Mr. Cornelius's room most days after I finished my lessons. My spelling grades had been high, and my final tests in arithmetic had been exempted. When Mr. Cornelius sent my report card home, Momma thought it was good, and then I'd been skipped over fourth grade, been promoted to fifth grade.

The next thing Miss Griffin did was order us boys to build us a toilet. I guess she had the school board truck some two-by-fours and planks and tin roofing to the edge of the field, but near the road, where we'd have to take an hour of time every day and put up the boards so we could pee where nobody'd see us doing it. She kept several hammers and nails at the school house, all of which she'd count before and after we'd spent an hour down by the field.

"It will be like you boys learning a skill," she said. I wasn't so sure I needed to learn a skill, whatever it might be, but I liked the idea of getting out of class for an hour every day. At least I did at first, until I found out about the meanness the big boys had in mind. Sometimes it got into my mind that Miss Griffin was using these "skills" as excuses to send mean kids out of her room. As the bullies aimed their devil meanness at us littler boys; an hour with them was puredee hell on us.

We grabbed our hammers and nails and waltzed across the road and gathered around the planks and boards like cowboys at a hanging in the moving pictures. At first, we nailed some two-by-fours together slaunchways and laid them on the ground. Looked like we'd built a fence to keep horny frogs from getting away. Some boys whose daddies built a barn or a shed said we had to put up some studs to nail your planks on. After two or three days we got the studs up, nailing every two-by-four catty-cornered every which way you can imagine. Then, by pounding a handful of nails in every board whether it needed them or not, as well as losing some in the grass, we ran out of nails. We missed a day at work until Miss Griffin brought a tow sack of nails to school.

The meanest boys behaved until we got enough boards up to keep prying eyes out. First, they didn't do any of the work. Next, they started pushing kids and pulling their arms up behind their backs. They cussed a lot. After a while, they hit us with sticks, anything to hurt. Most of us littler boys got to where we didn't want to work on our toilet and learn skills. Finally, Miss Griffin started to notice some of us had to be forced to go work, and she got suspicious we were lazy or she didn't know what.

"Why don't you want to work on the toilet, Leon?"

"I'm sick, I guess, Miss Griffin." She felt my forehead for fever.

It went on like that for several days. Of course, she couldn't go down there to the boys' toilet. Maybe she knew it was taking a long time to put one up, but maybe also she didn't care as long as the mean boys were out of the room. Even though we'd put up a toilet where people on the road couldn't see us pee, Nugene and the bigger boys made prisoners out of the rest of us, shoving and kicking us down to the trees in the creek, where they'd whip us with belts and scare us with long-blade knives. As usual, Melvin Junior got picked on, because of his red hair and saying Nugene was a ass. He even got tied to a tree with a belt where the big boys hit him with another belt. I stood there and hoped they'd run out of belts.

Momma got curious about why me and Melvin Junior didn't want to go to school.

"It ain't that far to walk," she said. She was pushing a heated iron over several shirts on her ironing board. It sounded like she was kind of joking.

"We don't mind walking. We just don't like getting paddled." I thought it was time we told somebody about the meanness.

She spit on her iron to see if it sizzled and set it back on the stove, took off her glasses and wiped them on her apron, and looked at me. One of her I-don't-mean-business looks on her face.

"Leon, what kind of mess you and Melvin Junior been up to?" Momma sure could look mad with her glasses off. "You'all supposed to mind your teacher and don't cause trouble." She put her glasses back on and put both hands on my shoulders. "I expect you to behave at school. I hear about your teacher having to spank you, I might give you another one at home."

"It ain't Miss Griffin spanks us. She don't do that," I said. "It's them mean big boys whip us with their belts." Well, I'd spilled the danger to somebody.

"That what you'all afraid to go to school for?"

"Yes'sum," I confessed.

Then she said what I was afraid she'd say. "You tell that teacher on them boys. They got no business whupping on you'all. It's that teacher's job to keep peace in school so kids can learn their lessons." She picked up the iron, spit on it again and shoved it along a shirt's tail laid on the ironing board. It smelled like smoke. "If I have to go over to that school at Christmas, I'll give her a piece of my mind, you hear."

Here was a case of me knowing better than my momma knowed. First time ever, I guess.

Melvin Junior had taken to beating up on cardboard boxes. He collected the boxes we'd brought our grocers home in and punched the living daylights out of them. On Saturday he punched and kicked a corrugated Post Toasties carton till it fell in pieces, and then he flattened a box that smelled like delicious apples and threw it in the air and hit it with his fist as it fell to the ground, where he jumped on it like a acrobat at the circus. I even give a try at punching a box that at one time held forty-eight rolls of toilet paper. It didn't take long to skin our knuckles till the blood showed.

"Dad gummit, that's the way I'd like to beat old Nugene till his nose bleeds," said Melvin Junior. He was mad as I'd ever seen him, and his hair is red, so you know.

By Sunday, all our knuckles were so sore we had to give the cardboard boxes some rest. We were sitting on the porch steps, gloomy over the idea of going to school next morning. My nerves were frazzled, Melvin Junior's brain was boiled, our knuckles were bruised. Uncle Bud and Mr. Waller had gone to the barn to be sure the stock were fed and had water. Momma was in the kitchen making some supper for us. We could hear her singing about bringing in some sheaves. The light from the kitchen lamps spread out onto the porch, a fan of yellow light that spread mine and Melvin's moving shadows out onto the yard. Otherwise, it was getting dark. Suddenly Melvin Junior slapped his hand against his knee, a noise sounding like a door slammed. He looked at me, best as he could in the dusky light.

"I'm gonna run away from home in the morning. You want to come along?"

Chapter 15

RUNNING AWAY FROM HOME

First thing we did to celebrate our freedom was build a fire and toast our peanut butter sandwiches. Poking them on a sharpened branch of a shrub we didn't know the name of, we held them in the flames until they smoked. The sandwiches smelled like peanut butter, but tasted like burning cardboard smells.

"Dang, I like cooking out in the open," said Melvin Junior. "Your food smells good and tastes like chicken and dumplings." He warmed his brogans near the fire. Uncle Bud had give him a soup-bowl haircut on Saturday, so his red hair stood up on top like a rooster's tail, and the razor's trim along the sides left enough bare skin to make his ears look cold.

"The pioneers didn't have it no better than this," I agreed.

We were stooping over a fire we'd made with sticks and leaves and kitchen matches down in a dry creek bed not far from the bridge usually occupied by Nugene's army. We'd dragged our feet and got to the creek well after school took up, which meant Delores and Doris

Jean had gone on to school with their book satchels, and we were getting ready to light out. Actually, we didn't have any detailed plans for our adventure beyond that of running away from home to escape the hell of New Hope school. It satisfied us knowing we'd make up a plan if we needed one.

"It might get a bit coolish at night," observed Melvin Junior, "but long as we got a roaring fire like this one we'll sleep on the ground next to it and be warm as a momma cat."

"I seen in a comic book where the Lone Ranger and Tonto took turns staying awake by their campfire at night. That way, no owl-hoots or panthers snuck up in the dark and made off with their life savings." I'd never stayed up all night in my whole life, but if the Lone Ranger and Tonto did, I guessed anybody could. I looked forward to being awake in the dark. There'd be sounds out in the brush, sure as you were born, cougars roaming around, but we'd listen real careful and gaze up at the stars. I'd always liked stars ever since old Lute pointed out the Milky Way to me when I was a little kid and I thought the moon was moving around the earth.

Since we were ready to light out, we covered our fire with sand and clods. Melvin Junior brushed out our footprints with a mesquite branch. No use letting trackers know we'd been here.

Of course, Momma'd be worried about us after we didn't come home, and I could just imagine her carrying on. I felt sorry for her, me being her only kid. Only thing was, she didn't understand what a hell our lives were like here at New Hope. Me and Melvin Junior didn't have no choice. What would anybody do if they were going to have their bowels cut out with a long-blade knife? Run, is what.

We didn't actually run. We carefully picked our way along a creek bed, not knowing where all it went. The creek was pretty dry, only once in a while muddy, even less often having puddles. All along the banks cottonwoods and willows and pin-oaks leaned toward the creek. A slight breeze moved and swayed their limbs. Most of the tree leaves had dropped on the ground, which walking on made a brittle, crispy sound as if you were stepping on Post Toasty corn flakes. We started to stomp and kick the leaves. The trees joined to make a covering above the creek bed, letting us see the pale sky through a patchy roof of branches.

"Ain't this more fun than school?" Melvin Junior liked the outdoors.

"Yep," I said. "But I wished we had a map that showed ever place we can go."

"Don't need no map to follow a creek," said Melvin Junior. No arguing with that.

Just then we had to stop quick. We both heard steps coming behind us. It was somebody in a hurry. The dead leaves gave the runner away.

"Hurry and duck behind them bushes," said Melvin Junior. "It might be the sheriff."

I couldn't imagine a sheriff after us, but I'd read in a comic book about a truant officer who'd catch runaway boys for a reward. My heart was pounding as I hunkered behind some red haw bushes and held my breath best as I could.

The runner stopped in front of my bush.

"Melvin Junior, what all you doing hidin' behind them bushes?"

I recognized the voice. It was Duane, a boy who lived on the other side of the main road. All we could do was come out in the open and look at each other.

If Melvin Junior had red hair, Duane had yellow hair. Or supposed to have. Once I'd heard Momma call some person "a dirty blond." That was Duane, whose family was poor like mine, and you could tell it by the way he wore patched clothes and skipped his Saturday bath. He had a little brother who'd pick buggers from his nose and eat them. But Kenny was friendly and not mean and tried to get along with other kids. Which was probably why he got picked on by Nugene's gang like me and Melvin Junior did. One time I'd seen old Duane wade out in a stock tank in the pasture near our school yard and rescue a soft ball another boy had hit over the fence for a home run. Now, he was standing in front of our bush looking like the orphan at the picnic.

"I heard you'all had run off to catch a freight train," he said. "That's why I come."

Melvin Junior crawled out of some scrub brush, picked dead leaves out of his rooster tail, and scrambled over to Duane. I stood up and watched them both, thrilled at how the story of our break out had picked up steam. The very idea of catching a freight train hadn't crossed my mind, but now as I thought about it, the more excited I become. It seemed so right. Sometimes at night I'd lie in bed and listen to some far-off freight locomotive whistle its way past a small town like Malone on its way to a big city, maybe Waco or Austin, and I'd dream about clambering on board and travel with it.

The look on Melvin Junior's face might have scared off most kids if they didn't know how he liked company for his mischief. I guess Duane read his expression pretty clear right way.

"I want to go, too," he said. "I asked to go to the toilet, and here I am."

"Depends, now," said Melvin Junior. "See, me and Leon, we tired out having to fight Nugene's gang every day. We can't put up with his bull any more. We figure to keep on the move until we come on a good job or get in the Army. People will be sorry we'd been in danger." Some of that was even news to me, but I could tell it hit the nail on the head for Duane.

"What we need is a good map," I said to Duane. "Sure, we can find our way by following the stars at night, if we have to." I wasn't too certain about the finer points of star reading, but I'd read about it in books, and it couldn't be all that hard. "You don't have a compass or nothing on you, I guess?"

"You'all let me tag along and I can do some guiding," offered Duane. "I know where this creek goes, up past the farm where Charles Kopecky lives, probably right up there past Dallas and Fort Worth."

"You been up there to Dallas and Fort Worth?" Melvin Junior wanted to know.

"Not all the way, but I been up past the Kopecky place."

That much of our expedition settled, the three of us set out along the creek bed.

I was the only one of us carrying a book satchel. Melvin Junior had left his satchel at home as he sometimes did, so Momma and Uncle Bud wouldn't be suspicious. Duane had run off and deserted his books and writing pads at school. Because my satchel caught on outstretched limbs, I had to slip the strap across the back of my neck and snake my arms through the strap and let the books bounce against my back. It was a bit of a pain the satchel bouncing on me like that, but the main book I had with me was one of those "Road to Adventure" books that showed a drawing of a ship steaming through the ocean on the cover. I could read from it at night after we built a log fire. No use in throwing it off in the bushes.

We come to a place where the creek split into two dry stream beds, both joining again in a little bit, which we saw made an island where briars grew thick as a tangle of barb wire. Probably the briars and brambles had chocked out any trees wanted to grow on the island. There was no water at all around the island, only a few rusty cans lay in a finger-shaped depression that once had been a mud puddle. My first thought was didn't we want to make a name for the island? Anybody in history ever come upon an island set out right away to give it a name. Hawaii Island. Rhode Island. Treasure Island. They'd all been named by ship captains and sailors whose boats wrecked up on the shore, mostly because they didn't have any maps.

I shucked off my book satchel and laid it on the sandy bottom of the dry creek bed.

"I suggest we name this island 'The Unknown Island.'" I waved my hand at the brambles along with my announcement.

"You got horse hockey for brains, Leon?" said Melvin Junior. "How can it be a unknown island when we know it's here?"

"We could call it 'Horse Hockey Island,'" suggested Duane helpfully.

"If you'all had any brains you'd know what's in them briars ain't no horse," Melvin Junior said. He started picking up a handful of smooth rocks from the creek bed.

"What?" asked Duane.

Melvin Junior tossed a rock at the thicket. A rustling of dry brambles was followed by a small rabbit bouncing out and running up the creek.

"It's a rabbit nest!" I shouted. Duane scrambled for rocks. Melvin Junior threw another one. I picked up somebody's old muddy shoe from the creek bed and flung it into the brambles.

Cottontail rabbits sprang out of the brush going in every direction. They bounced and leaped and ran off like steel ballies dropped on the kitchen floor. Every rabbit waved its cotton tail, and disappeared over the bank of the creek. We were still chunking rocks after they were long gone.

"Whew! That was fun," I said. "Gotta be careful, though. That could have been a cougar in the brambles." I looked at Melvin Junior. "A cougar would've et some of us."

"Probably would've et your little peter, you mean," he said. "They ain't no cougars left on this creek, dummy. People killed them off, treed them with hunting dogs, shot them out of the tree."

Duane had gone on to the other end of the island, and he came running back.

"Somebody's chopping wood up ahead of us. I heard their axe real loud."

That could be bad news for us. If it was somebody's daddy, they might turn us in.

What to do?

"In the Red Ryder movies at the picture show, they always send out a scout. Maybe we ought to send a scout up ahead. Scout out the land. Get back to us," I said.

"Only people Red Ryder ever scouts is Indians," said Melvin Junior. "That ain't no Indian up there chopping wood."

"I bet it's Mr. Kopecky," said Duane. "He lives just over there."

"That's Charles' daddy," I said.

Melvin Junior was studying the situation. "Since you know him so good, why don't you go up there and find out what he knows?"

"He might make me go back to school," said Duane.

"Come back this way if he does," said Melvin Junior. "Won't make no difference."

"You're already in trouble," I said. "A miss is as good as a mile."

Duane lurked off, hugging the brush line as if he'd be mistaken for a bush. Melvin Junior and I waited a few minutes and slunk after him, hoping to watch him scout Mr. Kopecky. We kept him in sight by hunkering down behind bushes and brush. Mr. Kopecky's axe was making the woods ring, though we couldn't see him at first. Our eyes followed Duane, who topped a small rise grown up with saplings. He disappeared in the direction of a tree falling to the ground with a loud whoosh and thump.

The axe chopping stopped, probably so Mr. Kopecky could figure out which branches on that tree to lop off. We waited for the chopping to start up again. We had to lay down on the ground and listen. It sounded like we heard voices coming from up there. I figured Mr. Kopecky was telling off Duane for wandering around on the creek instead of being in school. All me and Melvin Junior could do was wait. After a while I wondered why Duane was taking so long.

"You have any watch on you, Melvin Junior?"

"Don't need one. I tell time by the sun," he said.

"What time is it then?"

"Oh, it's about time you shut up and stopped asking questions," he advised.

"I only wondered how long Duane's been gone. You think he might be captured?"

Melvin got up, stooped, and peeked over the rise. "I think I see him coming. He's got something in his hand like he's eating."

Duane made his way through the saplings and slid down the bank. His mouth was moving like a little chopper. Crumbs of something stuck on his chin.

"So what did you find out? Can we get past the tree chopping?" Melvin Junior was hot to move on, get up to Dallas.

"I told Mr. Kopecky I was not in school, I was guiding some people on the creek." Duane looked embarrassed about telling a lie, I thought. "He didn't care if I skipped school. He said he'd done it hisself."

"It took you long enough," said Melvin Junior. "For a scout, you laid down on the job."

"He was eating his dinner. He asked me to have a sandwich."

"What kind of sandwich was it?" I was starting to feel empty myself.

"It was baloney."

"I wish you'd had some left," I said.

"It was good," said Duane.

"Hell, we better get going, or we won't get noplace," said Melvin Junior.

"I wish we could find someplace with baloney," I suggested.

Melvin Junior set off along the creek, walking bent over so Mr. Kopecky wouldn't spy him. Only thing was for me and Duane to follow. Because the creek bed was mostly dry, we hiked out good and easy. Melvin Junior stayed in front, Duane tried to stay up with him, and I came in last, thinking about baloney sandwiches. If I'd been in a comic book, there'd have been a cloud over my head, a baloney sandwich tucked inside, oozing salad dressing. I about tasted it.

"You'all stop a minute." Melvin Junior stopped still as a statue. He was looking up in a big post oak tree. I didn't know what he'd seen to make us stop. We'd been making good time for probably a half an hour. Walking right along, gaining on Dallas. "Look at what's in the fork of that tree." He pointed up there somewhere.

"I expect it's a squirrel," said Duane, craning his neck to look straight up. "Don't see nothing."

"Dang right it's a squirrel. Any you boys ever et squirrel?"

"Lots of times," said Duane. "My daddy shoots 'em, and my momma cooks 'em."

"Uncle Wylie takes his shotgun down on the creek and hunts all the time. We sure et lots of squirrel and rabbit at his house," I reminded Melvin Junior.

"If you'all stop blabbing, we could bang that sucker out of the tree with a rock, and have him for supper." Melvin Junior picked up a rock the size of a orange. Duane raced around, his hands picking and choosing rocks of all sizes. "Get ready to catch him when he lands on the ground." Melvin Junior was shouting.

I stood in the creek and watched what was going on. A thick forest of big trees grew up on one bank of the creek, while on the other bank it was mostly head-high brush and grass, and briars grew thick. I thought probably poison oak grew in that mess. Branches of the big trees and the willows leaned out over the creek nearly to the other side. Behind us the creek bed separated around the island and went out of sight. In front of where I was standing the sandy bottom of the creek led to a turning and wound out of sight. It looked a bit moist, even muddy, at the turning. On both sides of me Melvin Junior and Duane stood looking up into the branches of the big oak tree, their mouths popped open from the strain of staring upwards. Both of them wobbled rocks around in their hands. They waited for a squirrel to hop out on a branch in plain sight up there. *Kersplooey!* was on their minds.

Suddenly Melvin Junior heaved his orange-size rock upwards, possibly at a squirrel. The rock was heavier than he thought, because it failed to reach a high branch and fell dangerously back to the ground. Duane, thinking Melvin Junior had spotted a squirrel, popped several smaller rocks up into the dry leaves and branches where they bounced off and downwards. All squirrels had gone up the tree or inside it.

"Dang!" exclaimed Melvin Junior.

We decided to move on along the creek, hoping to discover something we could eat or turn into cash money.

"Remember that time we found a wallet in the road," I said for a hint about how much luck played a part in our lives.

"Yeah, it was made out of pasteboard and was empty as your head," said Melvin Junior.

"We tied a long string on it and laid it up on that bridge with the loose boards," I said, remembering the fun we had, "and when a car come along and stopped, we pulled it off the bridge and right out of a man's hand when he reached for it." I was telling it to Duane who had not been there.

"I guess you forgot how mad the man was and we had to run for our lives," Melvin Junior reminded me.

We strolled on around the corner of the creek, looking for some adventure or excitement. Me, I wanted a bank robber and his gang to show up, even a cougar at least. Duane had picked up a stick and dragged it on the ground and through the weeds on the bank, just making a noise. If a tall stalk of something like a dead sunflower stood on the bank, he whacked it down with his stick. Pretty soon he was thrashing around in any bunch of shrubs or vines we come across. Whack! Whack! Then a root he was banging away at began to move. It slowly at first drew up in a round shape, like the letter O, then quick as can be it whipped itself into the letter S, and began to glide over the sand toward us. It was a snake. A live snake. It was a brownish color, with dark green stripes along its back. You know how a snake seems to get longer the more it winds itself toward you? This one seemed to grow longer and longer. Its head was kind of flat, but you could see its tongue stick out and taste the air. Right away you knew it had poison fangs in its mouth.

"Get back! Get back!" Duane was shouting and jumping backwards.

"Hit it with the stick!" Melvin Junior tried to grab the stick. "It's a coachwhip snake!"

"Step on it! Grab it!" I'd become rooted to the ground, stunned by the creature's sudden appearance.

221

Melvin Junior wrestled the stick from Duane and struck the snake across the head, which caused it to stop and thrash its body back and forth. He hit it again several times, and the snake stopped moving except for a kind of whipping of its tail. Melvin Junior poked it with the stick, but it didn't move. We got closer, to see its stripes and fangs. White stuff oozed from its mouth.

"You killed it," said Duane, "but it ain't no coachwhip."

"It could be," said Melvin Junior.

"It's a chicken snake," said Duane. "They ain't poison, just get in the chicken house and load up on eggs."

"I think it's a grass snake," I said. We'd seen them around the pasture at Union High.

The dead snake was littler than the live snake. It didn't look so long now, maybe about four feet. I wanted to feel of it, see if it was scaly, and touched its skin, which was cold, but dry. I thought it was kind of pretty, close up. I didn't say it, because I knew it was dangerous. But I could hear Uncle Bud say, "It won't hurt you, but it'll make you hurt yourself." Which I guess we had kind of proved, the way we acted.

Melvin Junior turned the snake over on its back with the stick. The stomach was yellow and made up of ladder-like ridges which was probably its treads. It didn't have no legs to help it move over the ground.

"Don't leave it on its back. That would cause it to rain," said Duane. "I heard my daddy say that."

"If we wasn't running away from home, we could take it back to school and hide it in Nugene's desk," I suggested. "Maybe he'd sit on its fangs and turn him green with poison."

"Put him in that book satchel of yours and take him with us," said Melvin Junior.

That's when it come to me that I'd left my book satchel back there at the island. Our adventures had come so fast I'd forgot it.

"Well, let's thow him in the weeds, then." Melvin Junior and Duane were ready to move on. Time was getting short. Evening was creeping up on us, and we still didn't have any supper lined up. Fact was, I was getting one of the headaches I always got when I hadn't et anything. It was a sick headache that made me want to puke. I was thinking I hadn't made any plans for not eating when I ran away from home.

"Prob'ly I better go back and get my book satchel," I said. "Anybody finds it will know we come this way, be on our trail."

The other members of the gang decided they'd head on out, gain some miles on Dallas. I'd catch up with them by supper time.

When I got back to the island, I found my book satchel where I'd dropped it. First, I set down, pulled it up on my lap, and searched it, looking for any scrap of peanut butter and crackers I might find. There wasn't a salty peanut or a crumb, and I was starving, headache on the rise. Then I noticed my "Road to Adventure" book and tried to read some, settle my stomach, but my head hurt so bad my eyes swum, so I just set and listened to the noises in the trees and brush. A cottontail ran out of some brush and scampered back in when it saw me. Run for its life.

It was my sick headache that derailed me off the freight-train scheme and sent me back to school. Sick without anything to eat since we toasted our sandwiches, unable to fight the misery, I decided the only refuge was school and Miss Griffin. There was lots of things come into my sick brain. For one thing, it didn't occur to me to go home. Melvin Junior and Duane were still out there on the creek, so I couldn't squeal and get them in trouble. The truant officer would go after them with his blood hounds. It also come to me that Dallas might be a long ways off, more of a long haul than Melvin Junior and Duane would want to go on. It was possible they might back out and come back later on, so we could make up a story about being kidnapped or something. All I knew was anything you did somebody found out about it.

When I got back to school with my book satchel, the schoolyard was quiet. No yelling going on. All the kids had gone home. I took my heart in my mouth and stepped up on the porch. Miss Griffin was sitting at her desk reading some papers, and she looked up when I came in the door.

"Leon! I heard you'all were on a freight train gone to see the world."

"No, mam." I didn't know if she was laughing at us or serious. "We didn't get all the way there."

She took off her glasses and laid them on the papers. "You don't look so good. Come in and sit down at that desk." I was afraid she'd get a stick on me for being tardy, but she didn't. I must have looked sick, because she studied me pretty close for a bit. "Are Melvin Junior and Duane with you?"

"No, mam. They're still on the run to Dallas, last I saw of them." I figured I'd better tell her my true thinking on their grim fate. "I expect they'll be coming in after a while. We ran out of food, and killed a snake. I think Melvin Junior left it on its back, so it's likely to rain on them."

"I see," she said. "And why did you come back?"

"Miss Griffin, I got a sick headache from having nothing to eat since we toasted a peanut butter sandwich in a ditch. I didn't want to lay down and die, so I reckoned I'd better come on back to school." I hitched up my book satchel on the desk. "I couldn't find no scrap of food in my satchel."

She opened one of the drawers in her desk and took out a small bottle. From another drawer she removed a tin jug like you keep your coffee hot in. Out of the bottle she shook a pill, and then poured some liquid in a cup on her desk.

"Come here and get this aspirin and take it with some tea in this cup." She held out her hand. "You need to get over the headache before you can go home."

After I took the aspirin tablet, I laid my head on the desk and shut my eyes for a while. It was quiet in the room. I'd never seen it that quiet before. Usually there was some racket, mostly scufflings and talking. Now I thought it must be like this for the teacher every day after the kids go home. It passed my mind that this was the first time in my life I'd been alone in a school room with the teacher. With everybody gone, it was like Miss Griffin was not just the teacher but more like a regular lady. I got to wondering what her life must be like when she went home to supper. Did she have to go home and fix cornbread and red beans for her husband and kids? It was a funny way to think about a teacher. There was no way I could foresee that my teacher would get married within a year's time. Or that she would no longer be my teacher.

"Leon, I'm not going to punish you for skipping school," Miss Griffin said when she sent me home. "You did return to school and, besides, you seem to have punished yourself enough."

Me and my headache agreed with her on that. "However, Melvin Junior and Duane will have to answer to me when they get back. We know they had nobody's permission to go off." At that point I hadn't enough pluck to bring up their reasons for running away: Nugene's gang of murderers. "Those boys will have to stay in after school until Christmas to make up for missing their school work."

On the way home I found Melvin Junior waiting for me under the second bridge. That was the same bridge I had to wait under for him every day after school until Christmas. It was plain to both of us that if I was getting home an hour earlier than Melvin Junior every day, something had to be explained. And we didn't want to get into that. But as I was beginning to learn, somebody will always find out everything you do.

School programs was the closest thing to a party I ever got invited to. Not that I didn't know there was parties, because I read about them in comic books and *Life* magazine. Kids wearing paper hats like tee-pees ate birthday cakes nearly every time *Life* magazine come to a town. In comic books the people who loved parties more than anything you'd mention was teen-agers like Archie and Reggie. Just let Veronica or Betty even think about a party when they were supposed to be doing their arithmetic homework, and every teen-ager in a mile started begging to go and eat hotdogs and dance without any parents. But the Christmas program in 1942 at New Hope was the nearest I'd ever come to a real party. Of course, I could still remember the program at Cottonwood where I'd recited the poem about my dog, but that was more like school than it was about eating hotdogs or dancing. At Union High we'd had a Halloween night where you'd go and fish for toys behind a curtain. But the teachers called it a carnival, not a party. And the Japanese zeroes had bombed any chance of a Christmas party last year at Calina. So now Miss Griffin had notified our parents to bring presents and cakes and orange juice for a real Christmas party with a singing. You'd hear "Silent Night and Holy Night" and "Jingle Bells." I was pretty excited, most of all because I was old enough for a Christmas party to mean something.

Momma put on her nicest print dress and her coat-jacket and walked to school with me and Melvin Junior, helped us carry some tea cakes and popcorn balls she'd made. The main thing I was excited about was not so much the presents and candy the school trustees donated to us kids, but Momma going along and seeing our school and our teacher. She'd see for herself things I'd told her about. It always made a kid feel good when their momma visited school.

Us kids had dolled up the school room with cut-outs from construction paper that looked like stars and Christmas trees and sleigh bells, and hung them up around the room. The bells, of course, wouldn't ring, because they were paper fakes. There was a real Christmas tree, though. Somebody's daddy had cut it out of his cow pasture and set it up on a desk for us to hang silver icicles on. Under the tree laid a wrapped present for each kid, which mine had a bottle of hair oil, plus there was apples and oranges and stripy candy you never seen except at Christmas time and Brazil nuts you'd crack your teeth on. Of course, they never give out any fire crackers or Roman candles, which was useful things.

I noticed Momma talking to the grownups, there being lots of kids' parents at the party, as well as important grownups from the school trustees and all. Momma had gone to school herself with Doris Jean's daddy, Mr. Jack Loyd, who was a trustee, and maybe her momma also. Delores Pasley's momma and daddy, Mr. Albert Pasley, was there, and they lived on Mr. David's place too. Duane's momma and big sister had come, but we didn't mention the creek with its island and dead snake. It made me feel good that Momma seemed to have a good time and ate some cake. She seemed to enjoy the singing, but I didn't do any of it. I didn't know any of the words, only the names of the songs, tell the truth. After the singing come to an end, I saw Momma talking to Miss Griffin, which I guessed she was telling her about me and Melvin Junior being scared out of our wits. On the way home was when I found out what Miss Griffin told Momma.

Boy Howdy, was she mad. Like you'd figure, she genuine carried on.

"Leon, I am absolutely ashamed of you. What do you and Melvin Junior mean running off from school like that? Your teacher said the kids told her you'all'd run away from home on board a freight train. Now if that don't beat a goose a gobbling I don't know what. She said she been keeping you'all in after school ever day since, and I didn't hear nothing about it."

"It was Melvin Junior stayed in after school," I explained. He didn't say nothing.

Momma stopped in the road, shifted a sack of the stuff from the Christmas party to her other hand, and stared at me.

"Then where you been? You ain't come home by yourself."

"I guess I stopped under a bridge."

"Well, don't that beat all," she said. "You waited for Melvin Junior so me and Bud wouldn't find out what you'all done." She started walking along with the sack. "That's like you telling me some big story."

"No, mam, I didn't tell no story. I just didn't say nothing." I thought I could tell the difference.

"I don't know what I'm going to do with you, Leon. You can't stay out of school, or you'll be picking cotton the rest of your life. I try my best to work and keep you in clothes so you look decent as other kids do and go to school. You know it takes all we make working for Mr. David to keep up." She was going to make it worse than a whipping, I could tell. "I know if you'd had a daddy like other kids, you wouldn't get into meanness. You'd have a daddy to work for us, and he'd make you behave yourself and stay out of trouble." I wondered why Momma couldn't just take a stick to me and have done with it. "It's hard for a lone woman these days to raise up a kid by herself, I tell you." We walked on along, down the big hill, on past Delores Pasley's house, on across the laid-by cotton fields, and Momma never let up.

Melvin Junior was lucky. He only got a whaling with Uncle Bud's big belt when we got home.

Not long after the Christmas party we learned that next year we'd see some big changes at New Hope. If me and Melvin Junior hadn't run away from home and made Momma mad at us, then complain about our teacher we'd blamed it on, and tell the whole school board about the big boys, it might not have changed so much. Miss Griffin was going to get married, we'd have a new teacher, and

Nugene and his gang might have to leave school. They had got too big for their britches.

Another thing. Now, it looked like me and Melvin Junior had seen as much of the world as we were ever likely to. And another thing, Melvin Junior was talking about quitting school, and somebody told Momma I'd have to start riding a school bus to a high school at a place called Penelope, believe it or not. And still another thing, I found out my best friend would be a girl, named Peggy. But most of all, after running away from home it looked like conscience was gonna be with me from now own, and I'd probably have to grow up. That's what Momma said. She allowed I couldn't be a kid nomore.

A mess of cousins

Mr. Waller

This is the house I was born in,
and the remaining well

Daddy and Me

Momma and the Cotton Patch

Momma and Daddy in Blue Bonnets